When
Tomorrow
Speaks
❀ ❀ ❀ TO ❀ ❀ ❀
me

James Melia

ABOUT THE AUTHOR

Bridget Benson was born in County Mayo on the west coast of Ireland. A clairvoyant medium, she began working with the spirit at the age of three. At sixteen, she entered nurse's training, working in that field and using her gift for spirit contact to bring comfort to patients and their families. Since 1990 she has followed her true gift and vocation to the spirit world, seeing people from all over through word of mouth for readings, audiences, and interviews.

Bridget conducts public and private readings, appears at charity events, and uses her gift to help with police investigations. She has been a guest on numerous British television and radio programs. Visit Bridget online at www.bridgetbenson.com.

When
Tomorrow
Speaks
✿ ✿ ✿ TO ✿ ✿ ✿
me

MEMOIRS
of an IRISH MEDIUM

Bridget Benson
AS TOLD TO *Sophie McAdam*

Llewellyn Publications
Woodbury, Minnesota

First Edition
First Printing, 2010

Cover art © Johner Images/PunchStock
Cover design by Ellen Lawson
Editing by Connie Hill
Map © Chris Down

Llewellyn is a registered trademark of Llewellyn Worldwide Ltd.

Library of Congress Cataloging-in-Publication Data

Benson, Bridget, 1956–
  When tomorrow speaks to me :memoirs of an Irish medium / Bridget Benson
as told to Sophie McAdam. — 1st ed.
      p.   cm.
  ISBN 978-0-7387-2106-4
  1. Benson, Bridget, 1956–   2. Mediums—Ireland—Biography.   I. McAdam,
Sophie.   II. Title.
  BF1283.B46A3 2010
  133.9'1092—dc22
  [B]   2010025672

Llewellyn Worldwide Ltd. does not participate in, endorse, or have any authority or responsibility concerning private business transactions between our authors and the public.

All mail addressed to the author is forwarded, but the publisher cannot, unless specifically instructed by the author, give out an address or phone number.

Any Internet references contained in this work are current at publication time, but the publisher cannot guarantee that a specific location will continue to be maintained. Please refer to the publisher's website for links to authors' websites and other sources.

Cover model(s) used for illustrative purposes only and may not endorse or represent the books subject matter.

Llewellyn Publications
A Division of Llewellyn Worldwide Ltd.
2143 Wooddale Drive
Woodbury, MN 55125-2989
www.llewellyn.com

Printed in the United States of America

This book is dedicated to my beloved father, Charles, and also to my mother, Bridget, who passed to spirit on the 14th April 2010, aged ninety, sadly, before the publication of this book.

I feel blessed that they chose to be my parents, showing me the true meaning of strength and reassuring me that life is eternal and our loved ones are only a thought away.

I am not a professional author, so it is with much gratitude that I acknowledge the assistance of Sophie McAdam, journalist and writer.

CONTENTS

Prologue

I was three years old when I first saw Harry. I can picture him even now: his kind smiling eyes, his rough, weathered complexion, his craggy face creased with laughter lines. His presence made me feel safe and warm. Harry was probably in his seventies, but his full head of brown hair and clean-shaven face made him look younger.

He was dressed in a white pinstriped shirt and tweed mustard waistcoat, with turn-ups on his grey-green trousers, and his black boots were highly polished. He looked just like an ordinary person, like you or me.

After that first time, Harry never came back in the same outfit. There were times when he had braces on, and sometimes, to my amusement, he'd pair these with a belt. His trousers often looked a bit big for him around the waist and I remember wondering whether he'd borrowed them from somebody.

I start my story with Harry because things might have been very different had it not been for the messages he gave me in the earliest years of my life.

I'm Bridget Benson, clairvoyant medium. I've had the gift for as long as I can remember: since the first time I saw Harry one cold, winter's night at the tender age of three.

My gift has taken me from a ramshackle farm cottage in rural Ireland to appearances on TV, radio, and fundraising at high-profile charity events. My gift has saved me, burdened me, made me laugh, and made me cry.

This is my story—a story of ups and downs, twists and turns, joy and sorrow. I know that many of you will understand how it feels to lose a loved one, and I hope by sharing my story I can bring you peace, hope, and the knowledge that your loved ones are only a thought away.

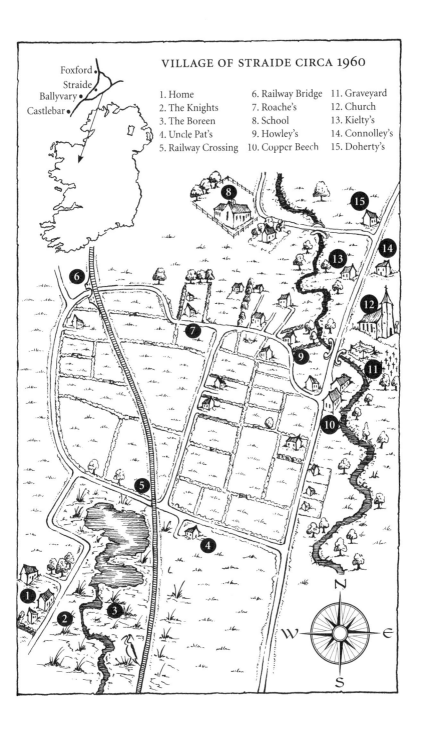

VILLAGE OF STRAIDE CIRCA 1960

1. Home
2. The Knights
3. The Boreen
4. Uncle Pat's
5. Railway Crossing
6. Railway Bridge
7. Roache's
8. School
9. Howley's
10. Copper Beech
11. Graveyard
12. Church
13. Kielty's
14. Connolley's
15. Doherty's

Foxford
Straide
Ballyvary
Castlebar

BASIC FAMILY TREE OF CLAIRVOYANT MEDIUM
BRIDGET BENSON

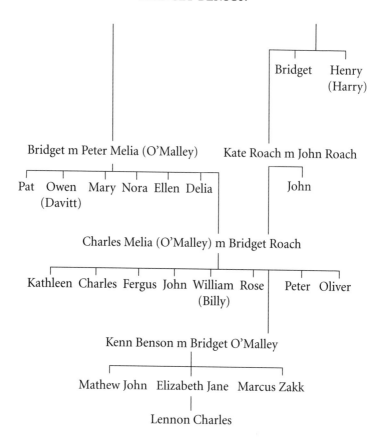

Bridget   Henry
(Harry)

Bridget m Peter Melia (O'Malley)   Kate Roach m John Roach

Pat   Owen   Mary   Nora   Ellen   Delia   John
(Davitt)

Charles Melia (O'Malley) m Bridget Roach

Kathleen   Charles   Fergus   John   William   Rose   Peter   Oliver
(Billy)

Kenn Benson m Bridget O'Malley

Mathew John   Elizabeth Jane   Marcus Zakk

Lennon Charles

PART ONE
A Very Different Child

INTRODUCTION

I was born in 1956 in the farming village of Straide, County Mayo, Western Ireland. Mayo is a county of lush meadows and peat bogs, purple heather-clad moorland, and sandy-beached lakes and rivers that make it famous for trout and salmon fishing.

The fertile land is broken up by hedgerows, clay pits, and craggy rocks of limestone and granite, while the Nephin Beg Mountains can be seen on the horizon where rolling hills meet the towering skyline. To the west of Straide is the Atlantic Ocean, where green fields give way to sharp cliffs that drop into sandy bays and secluded coves.

In Straide and its surrounding towns, farming is, and always has been, as natural as breathing. Today, even those who work in the nearby towns of Castlebar and Foxford still tend the land and peat bogs that have been passed down through generations for hundreds of years. Knowing how to make hay, dig turf, and farm cattle are essential life skills even now. In Straide, everyone is a farmer at heart.

Catholicism is deeply woven into the fabric of every community, but religion hasn't altered people's superstitious nature—traditional Celtic beliefs existed for hundreds of years before Catholicism came to Europe, so in Ireland it's common to find those who talk of fairies, leprechauns, spirits, giants, and banshees in much the same way as they believe in the Virgin Mary herself.

Until as recently as the 1970s, most families lived in small clay or stone homes topped with a thatched roof. Brightly painted stable doors would open into the cottage, where a stove sat in the huge chimney breast for cooking, heating water, and burning peat for warmth. A double bed, tucked into the wall and hidden by curtains, would stand by the fire, with a few wooden chairs and a small table pushed against the opposite wall for family meals.

Meat would be salted and hung above the fire to smoke, along with tankards, brewing cans, and oil lamps, while the cottage walls would be adorned with images of the Pope, the sacred heart of Jesus, and the Virgin Mary to bless the house.

This was the type of traditional rural home my elder brothers and sister were born into, but just before I came into the world my family moved from the railway gatehouse in Cloonclonlon where my mother was brought up, to our farm cottage in nearby Straide.

Built in 1955, it was a concrete, whitewashed bungalow with three small bedrooms and a kitchen and living area, which was the hub of the home.

Life was typical of rural Ireland at that time: we had no electricity, just open fires and oil lamps. Water was either collected through rainfall in a barrel at the back of the house, or by walking down the *boreen* (little road) to the village well. It was then heated on the range; in those days we had strip washes in the tin bath or nothing at all.

I was the seventh of nine children, so our house was always busy and hectic: small footsteps running across the floor, heavy iron pots banging on the stove, the chatter of adult conversation. When I think of home, I remember the bleating of the animals outside, often drowned out by the squeals of children playing or my father's laughter booming through the cottage.

My father, Charlie, was responsible for the running of the farm, while my mother, also called Bridget, stayed in the home: hand-washing clothes on the wooden rack, cleaning, cooking, and baking. Most of my earliest memories involve Mum standing at the range, churning butter, making jam and gooseberry pies from the bushes outside the house.

We had only a small herd of cattle compared to our neighbours, but we always had enough to sustain the family. We had ingredients from the farm—our own creamy milk and delicious homemade butter, and the hens for our eggs. Dad did the shopping in the small village of Ballyvary but we grew our own potatoes and every vegetable under the sun, so the only thing he'd ever buy was sugar, or flour for baking soda bread.

Red meat usually had to be bought as well, but there were times when snares were set in the field or at the back of the house to catch rabbits and hares. It took me years to realise that the chicken on the dinner table was the very same that had disappeared only hours earlier! I used to get very upset about that, but it was all part of farm life.

Our geese and turkeys were fattened up and eaten at Christmas too, and Dad always made black pudding from the blood. I remember him collecting it in an enamel bowl, adding pearl barley and seasoning, then wrapping the pudding in a cloth and leaving it to dry out for weeks in the pantry.

Though money was tight, we would have a proper meal every single night. My favourite was the traditional Irish meal of bacon, potatoes, and cabbage; the comforting aroma of sizzling meat and greens boiling on the range wafting through the cottage to welcome us home from school three or four times a week.

Dad was helped on the farm by my older brothers—Charlie, Fergus, and John, before they left for England along with our elder sister Kathleen. The rest of us had our part to play too—William (Billy), Rose, myself, and my two younger brothers, Peter and Oliver.

As well as my immediate family, the cottage was home to my maternal grandparents Kate and John Roach, and my Great Aunt Bridget, who had moved in with us from a farm lower down the valley before I was born.

There was no television in those days—at the most you would have music on the wireless, but usually children were forced to make their own entertainment. Rose and myself used to go Irish dancing and I was in the choir at school and church, which I loved.

There were lots of festivals throughout the year; midsummer dancing and bonfires on St. John the Baptist day in June, and of course St. Patrick's day, which was much the same then as it is now—lots of drinking and good fun!

For Easter, we didn't have chocolate, we got a hen egg, and I can remember for Christmas getting the odd little doll, but mostly it was just an apple and an orange—and that was something special. Rather than stockings, we used to have ordinary socks hung up at the bottom of the bed. There was never any mention of Santa Claus, and I don't recall seeing a Christmas card either.

Like everyone else, we were Roman Catholics and prayer was very important in our house: to thank God for both the beginning and end of the day. After our usual supper of gruel and the cod liver tablets we had to take every bedtime, the whole family used to say the Rosary around the table, tucked away against the kitchen wall. We would then kneel down by the side of our beds and pray for a restful sleep. Dad taught us to say:

"*Four corners of my bed, four angels on them spread: Matthew, Mark, Luke, and John, God bless this bed that I lay on. If I should die before I wake, I pray the Lord my soul to take.*"

It was after these prayers, once I was tucked up into bed with my brothers and sister, when my other life used to begin.

CHAPTER 1

Five of us slept in the bedroom at the front of the house: myself, Rose, Peter, and Oliver sharing a double bed (two at the top and two at the bottom), with Great Aunt Bridget in the single bed next to us.

When I was a child our room seemed very big, but in reality it was only the size of a pantry. The beds not only met in the middle but filled the room from wall to wall, leaving just enough room to squeeze through the door.

Dad would tuck us into bed: a big, cast iron four poster, covered in itchy, heavy blankets of every colour and description, and light an oil lamp. The smell of paraffin was comforting to me as a child, and the way the flames licked the inside of the glass lantern and cast a dull glow around the tiny space lulled me to sleep.

But I was usually the last to drop off, because night time was when Great Aunt Bridget talked to spirit. Every night, after my brothers and sisters had fallen asleep, I would sense a presence in the room and hear Great Aunt Bridget speaking in whispers. Peering out from under my blankets,

I would see her, propped up with cushions, in conversation with a spirit man who had appeared from nowhere and was perched on the end of her bed. I didn't know at the time that Great Aunt Bridget was clairvoyant—it never even occurred to me that her communication with these people at night was unusual, or that perhaps it should frighten me.

The spirit man was Harry, who had passed with tuberculosis before I was born, and he was brother to Granny Kate and Great Aunt Bridget. My aunt had never married, and had lived with Harry and her other brother Pat before coming to stay with us after they passed over.

Sadly, despite sharing a gift, Great Aunt Bridget and I never had a chance to develop a strong bond. When I was three, Bridget was already at the ripe old age of seventy-six—very elderly in those days. She was in poor health and confined to her bed, preferring to spend her days alone and emerging only for family meals. She was quite mysterious, a woman of few words, and would sit and eat her food very quietly before returning to bed. By the time I was five or six—old enough to understand my gift and feel the need to speak openly about what I was experiencing—Great Aunt Bridget's health had deteriorated rapidly and she had developed Alzheimer's. This meant she was often unable to recognize family members, let alone hold a conversation with me about the amazing gift we had in common.

Harry's real name was Henry, but in this life he was known as Harry, so that was the name he chose to communicate from spirit. I could see him as clearly as I could see my aunt and sleeping brothers and sister: he was as solid as anything else in that room. Harry was small in build and he didn't look like anyone else in the family; both my mother's and father's sides are tall and big boned.

He and Great Aunt Bridget would talk about their parents, their sister (my Granny Kate), and about life in general. And so it was that I developed my gift: each evening I would snuggle into my blankets and watch what I called "the play" unfold.

Usually I simply watched and listened as he spoke to Great Aunt Bridget. One night, however, Harry addressed me directly. Even though I felt totally at ease with this, the pandemonium that followed was the first time I realized I was different from my brothers and sisters.

It was pitch dark in the bedroom when Rose woke up and hissed, "Who are you talking to, Bridget?"

"I'm talking to Harry," I replied.

"Harry who?"

I paused, glancing from my sister to the man in front of me, whose presence was as clear as day. Harry smiled and looked from me to Rose. Why was she pretending he wasn't there?

"Can't you see him, at the bottom of the bed?"

Rose stared at me before whispering back, in a shaky voice: "No I can't see anybody. What's he saying?"

"He's talking away to me, can't you hear what he's saying? He's asking how we all are."

Rose dived under her blanket quick as lightning and immediately started screaming.

"Da! Da! Da!" She wailed, her body curled up and quaking under the bedspread.

At just three years old, I didn't understand what was happening. Why was she spoiling the play and trying to get me in trouble with Dad?

Rose's panicking woke my brothers up too, so by the time Dad arrived in the bedroom all three were crying and hysterical; there was an awful lot of commotion. Bridget was silent and expressionless—she continued to sit up in bed, simply watching Harry and keeping quiet. I often wonder what was going through her mind, but she was an enigma; I only wish I had been given the chance to ask her these things before she passed over.

As my brothers and sister continued to cry and squeal, I thought we'd surely be in for it now. But Dad didn't shout: he simply took a box of matches from his jacket pocket, re-lit the oil lamp, and placed it on the mantelpiece of our open fire.

"Come on now, that's enough excitement for one night," he said gently, sitting on the edge of our bed and pulling the rough blankets tight around us. "Now, Rose. There's nothing to be scared of."

She gave a final sob and laid down, Peter and Oliver doing the same. I sat defiantly and glared at Rose. Dad gave me a knowing look.

"Time for sleep now, Bridget. I'll speak to you tomorrow about this."

He never did confront me though; I found out as time passed that my father knew all about this world of spirit I had just discovered.

I remember Dad stayed with us until he thought we were all back safely to sleep, but even while he sat there, with the flickering oil lamp casting shadows against the small square window, I could still see Harry in the tiny room: he had moved to the window and was waiting patiently for things to settle down.

This was the night it hit me: my brothers and sisters weren't to be a part of the "play" like I was. I would never tell Rose when Harry came again. After that night, I would always talk quietly in whispers to him.

I knew Harry was Great Aunt Bridget's brother and that he couldn't be seen by my siblings, but I was yet to properly understand the difference between this plane and the spirit world. In my innocence I couldn't figure out where he appeared from—or disappeared to—in between his visits, and I remember asking Harry where he came from.

"*Not here,*" he answered mysteriously.

"You're not from Straide?" I asked, confused.

Harry smiled at me. "*Oh, I'm from Straide alright,*" he replied. "*Cloonconlon. But I passed over before your time, and when I visit you I'm coming from heaven.*"

I always assumed that heaven and Earth must be similar, what with Harry changing his clothes so frequently! But he explained that the spirit world has no need for material and physical things.

I'd know Harry was around if the room turned cold, but this would only happen for a moment: as soon as I turned and saw his friendly face, the temperature was back to normal. Spirits can take different forms; I asked Harry to visit me as a solid person so I wouldn't be afraid. So when he sat on the bed, I felt his hand when he held mine, as he often did to reassure me.

We spoke at all times of the day. People assume our conversations must have all been very important, but to be honest mostly it was general chit-chat. Saying that, he gave me some crucial messages, and a lot of our conversations revolved around my gift and how it would be used in the future.

Harry told me about passing over and how peaceful it was, and he would show me pictures in my mind of nurses' uniforms and babies: things in my future.

He'd tell me that I was going to see more as time went by, and how things were going to be different in my life: that I wasn't like my brothers and sisters.

"*They don't have what you have*," he once said.

"What *is* it that I have?" I asked him.

"*You have the ability to connect, to communicate*," Harry replied.

"With what?"

I hugged my knees under the thick blanket and waited with bated breath for his answer.

"*With another world.*"

He looked at me for a while and nodded slowly.

"*And you will go on to be known for that.*"

This news knocked me sideways with glee; I felt excited. Here was a man who could see into my future and was letting me know in advance. It was a wonderful gift to have, and the things he told me I couldn't imagine.

"*You will be known worldwide*," Harry predicted one time.

"*You will meet people of every colour, creed, class, and denomination.*"

I'm not sure I really understood a lot of what I was told, but thinking about it at night gave me shivers down my spine.

Unfortunately, Harry's messages often got me in hot water with Mum. I always wanted proof of things he had told me, and as a result I was very nosy as a child!

Mum used to keep things from Dad, probably to protect him from the stress. If money was tight she would write to relatives asking for money without his knowledge, and she would hide news that was seen as shameful—babies being born out of wedlock, for example. It used to drive Mum mad that often I'd know these things before she knew herself, and it incensed her even more that I would always go straight to Dad and tell him, *something's not right.*

"You're at it again, Bridget, and one day you're going to be in trouble for saying things like that," Mum would scold me. "Why are you telling him things I don't want him to know?"

"Well, because I'm being told," I shrugged innocently.

"You're not, you're just imagining it!" Mum would shout. "We always knew you were different; why are you like this?"

Then she would shake her head and storm out of the room, muttering under her breath that there was no point in talking to that child because she'd never learn.

My mother was very pious with her religion, and her reaction stemmed from the fact she didn't want any shame coming to the family. She was scared about what the villagers would say, and she didn't want to know what would happen in the future. Although she was a very loving, caring mother and met all of our needs, it always saddened me as a child that I couldn't discuss anything with her.

Instead, I turned to my father. He always told me the truth, never disputed anything I confided, and explained things to the best of his knowledge. But after every conversation he used to say, "But you haven't to tell people, Bridget. It's something people don't want to hear, and the priest won't like it."

I never understood why my being able to see and hear people from spirit wasn't accepted within my religion. I felt that God gave me my gift, so why was there a stigma?

We used to have to attend church at least three or four times a week. Dad, however, didn't go—I can't even recall him going to a funeral of anybody in the village. I never questioned this, but it turned out he'd had a fall out with the parish priest, Father McCarthy.

Catholics are expected to give a donation to the church every week, and Father McCarthy used to stand at the pulpit and announce how much each household had given. Being a big family, we couldn't afford to donate much, and

I used to find it shameful that it was called out for everyone to hear.

I remember sitting in the pew, my cheeks growing hot, my fingers twiddling the hem of my skirt nervously. I imagined the congregation going home to their roast dinners and gossiping about our family over glasses of *porta*, a traditional Irish spirit, laughing at how poor we must be and how terrible it was that my dad didn't ever turn up for worship. I kept my head lowered and my eyes on the floor, praying Father McCarthy would move swiftly on to the next donation, and that everybody was too busy daydreaming to be listening to him anyway.

I was terrified of Father McCarthy; he always seemed drunk and the smell of alcohol lingered on his breath. He had a slight slur that only people who knew him would recognise, and an arrogant swagger not suited to a man of the cloth. Maybe that's what put me off experimenting when I was older, because I've never been a drinker. There was always porta in the house and occasionally you'd see men drinking *poteen*, or "the hot stuff"—a very strong, illegal Irish spirit made with potatoes—but if my dad ever touched the stuff I didn't know about it.

Farm life was busy throughout the year and we all helped out with the chores. We had to be there when the cows were inseminated or taken to the bulls to be impregnated, and we had to watch and know by the phases of the moon when the calves would come. Dad was a firm believer in the ebb and flow of the natural world: he always used to say the cows "would birth this side of the new moon," and he was usually right.

I plaited the cows' tails and gave names to them: Blue-bell, Daisy, and Alice were my favourites. I adore animals and once came home with a stray goat some gypsies had left behind in the village, tethered to a fence at Straide church. Travellers were, and still are, a common sight in Ireland. Usually living in caravans and rarely staying in one town for long, travellers have wandered the hills and dales of Ireland for as long as anyone can remember. In much of Europe, they are considered a separate ethnic group, a nomadic people with their own customs and ways.

Although Dad understood why I had brought home the goat (he had always taught me the importance of feeding the earth and everything on it), Mum went mad with me for what she considered "stealing," and made me take it back.

Instead, I would catch bees in jam jars, removing their stingers so I could enjoy the sensation of them crawling over my hands. I collected frogspawn in spring and fed the birds my leftover gruel every day. I loved watching the pair of robins that visited our garden, and I would search for cuckoo spit in the fields, inspecting every stem and stalk for that white bubbly deposit, and listen out for its distinctive call.

Being a girl, my main role on the farm was to milk the cows—there were no machines in those days. I would sit in the cowshed on my tiny wooden stool, a tin bucket between my legs, and talk to the cows about anything I had on my mind as I squeezed.

Other chores included the harvest of wheat and barley; the ground was ploughed and prepared in winter and the seeds sown in spring. In summer the whole family helped to cut the crops with sickles, removing the grain from the chaff and threshing the corn, which was then used for baking bread. Sometimes we could stretch to pay our neighbour Martin Gaughan to come along with his combine harvester, but more often than not everything was done by hand.

The months of June to September were always the busiest: turf cut from the earth, the sheep sheared and crops weeded, cereals harvested, and berries picked. There was also the haymaking: grass was cut with a sickle then laid out in the sun to dry, turned constantly until it was ready and could be stored for the animals for winter.

I never felt alone as a child. By the time I was old enough to help with the farm chores I already had a small circle of spirit children as friends—and if I was out in the fields making hay, they would always be there with me. There was a Mary-Ann, a Patrick, and a Mary-Ellen. Then there was Mary-Ann's twin sister Lucy; I remember her more clearly than the others.

Lucy had a cheeky, pale face peppered with freckles, big green eyes framed by lovely long eyelashes, and her shoulder length red locks were always in pigtails. My hair was auburn at that time, and I used to try and wear it the same as Lucy's. She used to plait it first, and then once it got a bit of curl she'd take the braids out and have it pinned up with small clips at the side of her head.

Lucy shared a birthday with me and I was very fond of her. She was always friendly, and greeted me most days by swinging on the gate and saying, *"How are ya? It's nice to see you again!"*

The spirit children used to help me on the farm. Even my father used to comment on how quickly I stacked the cocks of hay compared to everyone else. After it was cut, it was turned with a pitchfork and piled into a huge haystack. Mine always seemed to go up and up and fit into place, whereas if my brothers and sisters were doing it, many a time it would fall over.

I welcomed in these friends and told them to come; I used to look so forward to seeing them. We used to sing together as we were working—mostly nursery rhymes, although there were a lot of songs they taught me that I've never heard anywhere else before or since!

When it came to stacking the turf peat, I felt again that my spirit friends were physically helping, even though it would have looked to anyone else that I was alone.

Turf peat is rotten plant material, formed five thousand years ago when the very first farmers chopped down the forests and left the ground vulnerable to the wet Atlantic climate. Peat is traditionally what Irish people burn in their open fires, for cooking and warmth.

The vast expanses of peatland are known as bogs, and every family had their own plot of land to dig peat from huge trenches cut deep into the ground. All over the moorland above Straide, hundreds of these trenches are carved from the land for as far as the eye can see. Even today, most rural people have their own family bog—a trench passed down through generations. These historic bogs won't last forever: in most of Europe they have long been used up for fuel; but in Ireland, especially in the west, they remain for now.

Our bog was miles from home in the moorland over-looking Straide. The sods were cut from the trench by hand with a *slane*, a spade shaped to allow two sides of turf to be cut at the same time.

These blocks of earth were then stacked in small piles, turned regularly to dry in the sun and then piled together in an enormous tower until autumn, when we brought the dried fuel home in *creels*—big weaved baskets attached with a straw rope over the donkey's flanks.

I would be in the bog from eight in the morning until ten at night, and my spirit friends would keep me company throughout these long summer days.

When I wasn't busy with the farm chores, I would sit talking with Lucy and my other spirit friends in the veg-etable patch at the front of the house. The spirit children would eat Dad's carrots, cabbages, and turnips, and I would join them: I had a thing for eating scallions, or spring on-ions, as fast as they were growing.

One time, I was sitting in the vegetable patch with my friends when my neighbour, Mick McCormack, asked who I was speaking to.

"Mind your own business and I'll mind mine, kiss your own sweetheart and I'll kiss mine," I told him brazenly, without a pause.

Mick looked at me with amusement, as if to say, *where's that coming from, out of your mouth so young?* My spirit friends were rolling around laughing at my cheekiness, and I giggled at our shared joke as Mick walked away, shaking his head in astonishment at this peculiar child before him.

I loved all my brothers and sisters, but I didn't get the same sense of happiness playing with them as I did from these children who came to visit me. I felt increasingly misunderstood and unable to open up around my brothers and sisters, whereas playing with the spirit children enabled me to be myself and feel happy and at peace with my gift.

The little lads wore knee-length socks and khaki trousers often covered in tweed patches, with peaked baker boy caps. I used to envy the girls' fashion; they always seemed as if they were in their Sunday best and they looked so sophisticated and pretty to me. They wore thick stockings and skirts that skimmed their calves or ankles, with tight, high-collared blouses and lace-up boots.

The difference in clothing always made me feel as if they weren't of my time, so I presumed as life went on that these were children who had lived in the village long ago, probably in Victorian times. This made sense because one of our fields was a children's burial ground, or *kileen*: we called it the giant's grave; when I was young I took that literally and used to imagine an enormous man lying under the earth.

No one is sure of the story behind the mass grave. My relative Kate Knight is now eighty-four and still believes, like many others in the village, that a giant was walking through the fields one night and fell down dead in that spot. Others say it is full of babies who died before being baptized; but more likely it is one of many ancient Celtic tombs that litter the Foxford way and whose history is unknown.

Nowadays there is a plaque in the field to commemorate the children buried under the ground, but when I was growing up it was simply local knowledge that it housed the bodies of young children and we were forbidden from touching it. But to me, there was nothing to fear from children who had passed, and the giant's grave was another place I liked to sit, laughing and talking to the children no one else could see.

My other favourite spot was under the gooseberry bush at the front of the house. I'd once asked Dad where I came from and he jokingly told me I was found there, so from that day on I'd sit under the bush with a little green hat and coat he'd bought for me, playing with my spirit friends— and the fairies who lived there.

The fairies were just as you'd imagine; like human butterflies. They had gossamer wings and long glossy hair, usually black, and they fluttered gracefully about the bushes surrounded by a beautiful golden aura.

The fairies were accompanied by leprechauns too, a race often thought to be mythical but very real to me as a child. They lived alongside the fairies, eating berries and sleeping on the moss. Sometimes the leprechauns would hop up on to my window ledge and beckon to me to go outside. The clichés are true; the leprechauns were no bigger than two feet tall and wore uniforms of green, with black hats and buckled belts. Facial features and hair colour were different from one leprechaun to the next, but they all loved to sing and dance in a circle.

It is impossible to describe the music of these tiny people: our language wouldn't do it justice. Their voices are otherworldly, the sound they make isn't human, and no comparisons can be made to anything we may hear to on the earth plane. All I can describe is the way their songs made me *feel*: ecstatic, joyous, filled with love and peace—it was a very deep spiritual experience.

One night, I was watching their campfire burning through our kitchen window, when Dad sidled up to me and gestured outside.

"Are you watching the little men?" He asked me with a grin.

I looked at him, wide-eyed. "You can see them?" I gasped.

" 'Course I can see them," Dad replied. He nodded over at the tiny people outside. "They wear a cap like I do."

I giggled. Dad never went anywhere without his peaked cap. He had lots of thick brown hair, but he used to say a person's head was the most important part of the body and had to be kept warm. I used to take his advice very seriously and make sure wherever I could that I would be wearing a hat—so I'd sit under the gooseberry bush with my little green cap perched on my head, or if we were going down to the bog to work I'd wear a headscarf, *or plaikeen* as we called them.

CHAPTER 2

Dad was older than Mum by nineteen years. They met while he was working at the railway house for my grandparents; she was only a girl of twelve at the time. He once told me that he had known the second he laid eyes on her that they would marry—information I found quite disturbing at the time, but which I now know was simply another of my father's predictions. He paid her no attention, of course, being a child as she was, but when she was sixteen she fell in love with him. He waited until she was twenty-three to give in to her advances, and they married that same year, July 1943, when Dad was forty-two. Perhaps it didn't seem so strange to him because his own parents had a similar age gap: his mother was older than his father by seventeen years, and on top of that, on my mother's side, Granny Kate was eighteen years older than her husband, my Granddad John!

The obvious downside of my parents' age gap was that by the time I was born, my father's health was suffering. He had diabetes and arthritis, so my older brothers had taken on most of the running of the farm and Dad was able to spend more time with us at home.

Dad always occupied us because he could play the harmonica and the tin whistle (a traditional Irish flute), and our neighbour Mick McCormack used to play the accordion, or *squeezebox* as it was known, so there used to be music and activities taking place in the house. Mick, along with another neighbour, Jim Smith, used to bring *porta* to our house and sit around the table with Dad, playing traditional Irish folk songs while we would sing along. Those gatherings are some of my fondest memories: the wonderful sound of the instruments as the fire roared in the hearth, my siblings and I gleefully banging on the table in time to the music or jigging around the kitchen in fits of giggles, the laughter of the men as they clinked their glasses and drank their *porta* between songs.

I love to hear people talking about Dad; he was such a character. He was born in 1901 and he often talked about how hard those times were. Around 1.5 million Irish people left for America and the hope of a better life at the turn of the century, and my dad's sisters Mary, Delia, and Ellen were amongst them. Dad's only dream was to visit them over the water before he died, which sadly never happened.

Growing up in this era—only fifty years after the end of the Great Potato Famine in 1848—gave Dad a sense of how important it was to never waste anything—so although he was very generous, he was also very strict about us clearing our plates and being grateful for the food in our bellies. We did get sweets every week though, which back in the 1960s was a lot. Every time he went shopping he brought back chocolate bars called *Billy Bolands* for us all, and Emerald chocolate caramels for Mum.

My parents were very much in love. My dad is remembered in the village for being "sound as a bell and a great provider for his family," and my elderly relatives fondly recall how much he adored my mother. But although they were best friends and soulmates, my parents were like chalk and cheese: especially when it came to the subject of my gift.

I once overheard a conversation between my parents; Mum was worried about me talking to myself all the time and wondering whether they should call Father McCarthy in to get me blessed. They were in the kitchen while Mum was making gruel and I was coming in from feeding the chickens.

"I'm just saying, Charlie," I heard Mum say, a pan banging on the stove.

"It's not right, all this talking to invisible people, and it doesn't give a good impression."

I heard Dad sigh and sensed his unease at being caught in the middle of Mum and I.

"She's different alright," he replied. "But I don't know, Bridget. I really don't think it would help matters."

Now it was Mum's turn to sigh. I heard her bustling around the room, thinking about what was best. "I'm just worried about her, that's all," She answered finally, slamming down another pot on the range.

There was a silence and then I heard Dad's footsteps move towards Mum, and the sound of a reassuring kiss being planted on her head. "She's a good girl, our Bridget," Dad told her gently. "She's going to be just fine."

I think it's fair to say I felt like the black sheep of the family: if it wasn't for the support and unconditional love of my doting father, my childhood wouldn't have been quite as happy. I wasn't quite sure whether being different was good or bad—Mum's attitude was one of shame and frustration, while Dad and Harry compensated for this and made me feel special. But either way, as I was constantly reminded by Harry and my parents, I was very different to my siblings.

Kathleen, being the eldest, was very responsible and seemed to take the role of an adult in the house. As his first born, my father adored her and she could do no wrong.

I remember when my brother Oliver was born in 1959; Kathleen had me going out collecting hen eggs to make a cake as a celebration for him coming home from hospital. She used seventeen eggs to make this cake—every egg in the house—and it just flopped; Dad was going mad at her for wasting our whole weeks' supply. That's the only time I ever heard him telling her off, and Kathleen was crying because it was the first time she'd ever baked anything.

But then Mum came home, tired but radiant, and brought back this beautiful child with the jet-black hair, and it was all forgotten. Dad was overwhelmed, I remember the tears in his eyes, and Kathleen was over the moon.

She could be an absolute sod though. There was a lad in the village called Mickey Smith; we used to call him Mickabilly. His dad was Jim Smith, the man who played the tin whistle with Dad. I nicknamed him Long Tall Jim due to his thin, wiry frame and long black coat.

This Mickabilly used to really torment Kathleen, so one day she decided to get him back. She invited him into our house, where we'd just painted the doors and window frames, and picked up this can of red lead gloss. Then Kathleen pinned Mickabilly down and painted him from top to bottom, laughing and saying he was a "red Indian." The gloss was all over Mickabilly's eyes and mouth and I remember he was squealing for help.

I can still see Jimabilly coming down the road to talk to our Dad. He was really giving off, shouting that he had come to sort out what my father was going to do to Kathleen for painting his son. Kathleen was hiding in the bedroom, laughing her head off.

Another time when I was about six, I wouldn't go to the well like she'd asked, so she locked me in the cow shed. She was much bigger and stronger than me, so it was easy for her to pin me down, even as I struggled and kicked, thrashing around and begging her to let me go as she sat on my arms and tied rope around my wrists. Kathleen attached the rope to the wooden posts in that jet black hole and wouldn't let me out for ages. I was screaming and crying the whole time, but it taught me a lesson: when she asked me to do something after that I would do it; there was no hesitation!

Rose was very different; she wouldn't say boo to a goose. We were opposites, and never close—I was very boisterous and inquisitive, while Rose was quiet and did as she was told.

Billy was born prematurely and was a sickly child; he couldn't risk getting cold due to his bad chest and was wrapped in cotton wool as a result. Even though he didn't get as many chores as us and was kept back in school, Billy was something of a genius in other ways—he could always memorise car registration numbers, for example. But he was incredibly sensitive and always bursting into tears. Mum "kept him back"—meaning she didn't allow him to marry—as is often the tradition in Ireland with a child from each family, to look after their parents in old age. He lived with Mum, as her full-time caregiver, until her passing earlier this year.

Peter was a good-looking lad and very mischievous: like Kathleen, he could be a sod and was forever playing practical jokes and getting me in trouble.

One birthday, my dad had taken me to buy a new dress. This didn't happen often and I was in love with this beautiful, flowery frock—I didn't want to take it off, even though we were making hay in the field that day.

Peter dared me to jump across a swamp and then stuck his foot out and tripped me up. I fell straight in and couldn't swim; I was drowning and Peter had to help me out with a hayfork, still giggling as he did so. I was in floods of tears and ran home with wet hair, the new dress sticking to my cold body. Mum gave me a good whack for that one.

Another time, Peter and I were picking mushrooms. He sent me to pick a big mound of fungi stuck to a fence; only it was a bees' nest and I was stung really badly: Peter knew all along, he was killing himself laughing.

Oliver was quieter and more serious than his elder brother, but they had similar looks. Oliver was a beautiful child, with big brown eyes, clear skin and dimples in his cheeks. As the baby, he was Kathleen's favourite and the only one of us she ever bought presents for—the rest of us got hand-me-downs.

Kathleen, along with Charlie, Fergus, and John, left for England to find work at quite a young age. At that time, a lot of Irish people emigrated in their teens because there wasn't enough on the land to feed everybody, and there wasn't enough money to make.

Mum used to spend a lot of time upset about my brothers and sister being in England; it was really distressing for all of us having them so far away. I used to sit glumly looking out of the window, imagining them in their homes across the water. It seemed so far away, so very different in my mind to Ireland. I pictured hundreds of people, different colours and creeds; I pictured a huge country with no countryside, and strange houses with staircases and different food.

Castlebar was the nearest station to home and you could see the railway from our land, its track cutting neatly through the lush green fields. The steam trains used to chug past our cottage on their way, billowing smoke pouring from their shining chimneys.

Watching them chuffing up and down the line, I used to hope desperately that my brothers and sister were aboard. I'd stand down on the line, heart pounding with excitement as a train appeared in the distance, its horn sounding, the metal of the railway track nearby juddering in anticipation. It was always a brown trunk they had packed, and they would never stay longer than two or three weeks.

Dad coped with it better than Mum, but he did used to cry a lot for Kathleen. She was his first-born and favourite child, at least she was before she left and I took over as his confidante. Kathleen had previously brought money home from her job in the Castlebar hospital as an orderly, and I remember her buying clothes for Oliver, the baby of the family.

Once she was in England, Kathleen used to go to jumble sales—an English tradition of selling unwanted goods on table tops in the church hall or community centre—and send clothes home for all of us. It was always exciting to see the postman in his short, buttoned black jacket coming up the *boreen*, a parcel made from potato sack and tied with string sitting in his bicycle basket.

My siblings and I went to St. Peter and Paul Straide School. It was, and still is, a concrete building, painted cream and eggshell blue and set on a narrow road leading to the maze of *boreens* and farmland beyond. The concrete wall at the school's entrance was broken by two stiles for the children to hop over into the grass surrounding the building.

Before school we had prayers to say and chores to do, and in the winter we would have to bring hay to the cattle before setting off on the four- or five-mile walk. It was often bitterly cold and we would wear socks on our hands, blowing on them to keep warm as we hurried along. My teacher was called Diarmuid O'Shea and every morning he would cane me, two slaps on each hand, for being late.

I can still feel the sharp sting of that stick as he brought it down on my palms, the crack of it echoing around the classroom, his dark eyes glinting, his face expressionless. Despite his poker face, I always sensed that he enjoyed this sadistic daily ritual, and I forced myself to be stubborn and show no emotion.

As the tears sprang to my eyes and my hands burned as though on fire, I willed myself not to show it and to concentrate on happy thoughts: speaking to the fairies under the gooseberry bush, Dad scooping me up in his arms as I ran into the cottage that evening, a hot meal waiting for me on my return, and, when the winters were particularly bad, the fact that the cane helped warm up my frost-bitten hands.

Every single household had to bring peat for the school fires. The children who brought their peat were allowed to sit in front of the open fire, warming their hands and their glass bottles of steaming tea, but those who didn't had to drink it cold and sit at the back of the room, shivering.

More often than not, I fell into the latter category. With Dad being ill and struggling to get in and out of the cart, we sometimes found it difficult to get the peat on time. Mum used to prepare our bottles of hot tea— glass jars stuffed with a cork of newspaper—and bustle us out of the door with our sandwiches of cheese or corned beef wrapped in brown paper.

By the time we arrived at school after the long journey, our hands were blue and our tea undrinkable. I remember vividly the feeling of shame and humiliation as I was sent angrily by Mr. O'Shea to the back of the class, segregated from my friends who had the means to bring their peat.

I was closest to Margaret Dunbar, Maureen Maloney, and Marion Carney. We four always stuck together, along with Mary-Rose Kelly who was in a different class. But even though they were my best friends, I learned from a very young age that it wasn't wise to discuss my spiritual experiences with them.

For example, I could always see "extra" people around the school: I can't remember a time when it was any other way. It is difficult to explain (particularly when spirits usually look like solid people) how I was aware they were not of this earth plane. Sometimes it was in the way they seemed only to make contact with *me*, whether this was through knowing looks as they met my gaze, or telepathically, by speaking to me in my mind. Other times, it was in the clothes they wore, or something unusual about their mannerisms and appearance that was not of our time.

Usually though, it was simply the fact that I noticed nobody else could see them. My classmates would run around the playground squealing, playing hopscotch, or skipping or chase, oblivious to the spirit children blocking their path or playing their own games nearby.

In addition to seeing spirit children on a daily basis, I had a recurring supernatural experience with another teacher, Miss Malloy. Unlike Mr. O'Shea, she was young and slim, with soft features and short dark hair. She was very kind to us, and if it were very cold or wet she would sometimes take us halfway home to Kelly's Cross in her green Morris Minor.

Sometimes I'd be looking at Miss Malloy as she stood at the blackboard addressing the class, and her features would slowly begin to morph into somebody else's. I watched in fascination, wide-eyed, as her tweed clothing was replaced by that of a Victorian lady: a high-waisted flowing black skirt, a lacy white blouse buttoned up to the neck, and a plaid shawl pinned together with a brooch. This experience happened regularly, usually lasting five or ten minutes. I was never afraid of what I saw, nor did I question it much—I simply found it all very exciting.

My gift meant that I wasn't able to concentrate properly at school, and I did mention my experiences a few times to my school friends. Sometimes people expressed an interest, but other times my stories were met with raised eyebrows and shared looks as if to say, "*She's a funny one, that Bridget O'Malley.*"

I never got the impression my classmates thought I was lying, but at the same time I realised they didn't understand: there were certain things that I had to keep to myself. Of course that makes a child feel quite alone, but I took comfort from the fact I had my spirit friends to speak to—I made a decision at a very young age to separate my two lives.

As well as the familiar spirit friends I'd grown accustomed to, I would see lots of others on the walk to and from school.

There would be at least twenty children walking to school along a narrow dirt track lined with trees, so we used to hurry as fast as we could. You couldn't walk that route now because of the flow of the traffic, but in the 1960s we hardly ever saw a car—just horses and carts and people on bicycles. I used to get in trouble for walking barefoot; I found it really difficult to wear shoes. I just couldn't stand my feet being enclosed, and I felt much freer and connected to nature without them.

There was one old house on our route that was a bit of a tumbledown shack, abandoned and empty—or so everybody thought. But while the other children chattered away as we hurried past, I used to glance warily over at the house and see people wandering around inside, or sitting on the porch watching us pass. Like most of the spirits I saw, they were always dressed in Victorian clothes, and they would look at me with cool expressions—as if I was invading their time and space by noticing their existence.

That house used to send shivers down my spine, but there was another unoccupied house we had to pass which petrified me even more: it was well known to be haunted and had quite a reputation in the village. The atmosphere surrounding it was stifling and oppressive, and the blurred expressions of the people I could see looking out of the dirty, cracked windows made my heart race with fear: cold and angry, dark and brooding.

After passing these houses, we would come to Bob Maury's farm. We were so hungry after school that we would dare each other to sneak into his orchards and steal apples and a drink of water from his well.

Bob Maury was a small man, and he used to wear a tweed waistcoat and some dirty old trousers held up with a piece of string. He had thin auburn hair covered with a flat cap, and his Wellington boots were always turned over at the top.

Bob wasn't a particularly nice man, and more often than not he would be hiding somewhere to catch us in the act of apple picking. He would give us a good belt with whatever he had to hand, whether it be a fork, spade, or stick. I did it once, spurred on by my friends, but I got a really good clattering from him and never tried it again!

There were four shops on the way to and from school—Hynes', Kielty's, Connelly's, and Doherty's, and most days after school we'd pile into the shop, our mouths watering at the delights in their big glass jars: chocolate orange sweets, emerald chocolate toffees, aniseed balls, and chocolate limes.

Connelly's was the best because they would let you have things "on tick," or paying at a later date—we'd get a lolly on the Monday and pay for it on Tuesday; they trusted us to pay it back and we always did.

When we walked home from school on the low road we could see our house on the horizon, and I can always recall my father standing at the gable of the house waving to us. I'd wave back excitedly and on nearing the house I'd break into a run, galloping as fast as my little legs would go until I'd reached him and he'd caught me in his arms, swinging me around and planting a big kiss on my grinning face.

CHAPTER 3

On my seventh birthday, in 1963, I woke with a bad feeling. The house seemed empty and cold, and I had searched everywhere for Mum until finally I dashed into the last place I could think of: the bedroom where Grandma slept.

Although we had yet to be told, somehow I already knew that Grandma had passed. I know now that her kidneys had failed, but at the time we weren't told she was ill, so her passing felt very sudden.

Granny Kate didn't look her age, but it was her time to go. She was ninety-four, though I can't recall her seeming so elderly. At five foot ten, she was very tall, big-boned and strong, with not a scrap of fat on her.

I found Mum lovingly tending to her body, making her ready to go into the coffin for the wake. Mum wasn't crying; she looked sad but composed, holding a towel and washing Granny Kate's face with soapy water from an enamel bowl.

Granny Kate was wearing a traditional full-length rusty-brown habit made of rough material, with an ivory frill at her chin. She looked like she was just taking a nap.

I stayed for a moment, staring in shock, and my eyes met Mum's. She said nothing but looked furious that I'd broken such a private moment. They were very close; Granny Kate's only other surviving child, John, had gone to Scotland before I was born and never returned.

I think Mum was worried about the effect seeing a dead body might have on me as a little girl, but I was only worried about how devastated she seemed at Grandma's passing, especially having lost my Granddad John too. He had passed over the previous year, aged seventy-six.

Granddad John had been a man of few words; he would wander around the house but never intruded on Mum and Dad's privacy. He taught me how to shave him with a cut-throat razor, and I remember his strange habit of always using a knife to cut his toenails. On one occasion, he got an infection which quickly turned to gangrene. He had his leg amputated below the knee, then died in hospital from a stroke.

Harry had told me after this that Granddad John was with him, and I had passed on this message to Granny Kate. She hadn't said much, but I know that she believed me: I found out recently through my brother Fergie that she knew she was going to pass, and had no qualms about it at all.

But Granny Kate was never the same after losing her husband. She seemed so alone, and I would make a point of spending more time with her. Granny Kate was a character: she always had digestive biscuits hidden in her room, and I remember her rubbing germoline on her legs "to stop inflammation," and eating *imps* to keep her bowels working. She wore rouge on her cheeks every day but refused to wear her teeth, and she smoked a pipe.

Granny Kate played a very big part in our upbringing. I remember how she used to help Mum with the cooking and then make some beautiful potato cakes with the leftovers. My siblings and I caught on to this and deliberately used to leave our potatoes so she would make the cakes—we seemed to get away with a lot with her.

She was very easy-going, the storyteller of the house. We used to spend a lot of time down in the room talking to Granny Kate, and I did confide in her a lot about my experiences. She was a believer, but like everyone else, she also told me it wasn't something I was supposed to discuss, so I never pushed her to tell me more.

Nevertheless, she did speak of healers in the village, and how she could hear the banshee's cry—Irish folklore of a wailing lady, her terrible scream carried by the wind—traditionally, her screeching was a signal that someone had died. I could always hear this awful noise too, and it was usually discussed in our house just before there was a knock at the door to confirm the sad news of someone's passing. Even my mother talked about the banshee, so I began to assume that everyone must see and hear the same as me—it was just that I was more brazen in speaking about it.

Granny Kate's coffin was set on a stand in the kitchen during her wake. It was a typical Irish Catholic affair; villagers congregating at the house to offer condolences and play music, drink *porta* and tell stories.

Laying in her coffin, it was the first time I'd ever seen Granny Kate without her trademark beret—she had thick, long hair down to her waist, and every day she would plait it and roll it around the top of her head, tucking it carefully under a black beret. Both Granny Kate and Great Aunt Bridget wore these berets and were rarely seen without them. Because of that I'd never seen her hair loose, and I remember thinking how lovely it was: mousy brown rather than grey.

After Granny Kate passed, I missed the woody smell of her clay pipe, its blue haze filling the parlour. I remember when I was about six; I'd watched Granny Kate kneeling on the floor and rolling up a newspaper to light her pipe from the open fire as she always did. Curiosity overcame me and I copied her when I was alone, but a piece of coal fell into my Wellington boot and burned through the rubber into my foot. It was agony and I screamed the place down; Mum came running into the room in a panic and pulled the boot off, ripping away all my skin in the process. I still have that scar today, but it taught me never to smoke again!

Granny Kate had a beautiful funeral and looked very peaceful, but I found her death, and particularly the timing of it, very hard to deal with.

My birthday should have been a happy event, one that I had been looking forward to for months. Now, rather than a celebratory occasion, there was an atmosphere of glumness and grief. I'm ashamed to say I was quite angry with my grandmother: in my childish mind, still trying to understand the way the spirit world worked, she had *chosen* my birthday to leave us, and I struggled to understand why this was. Of all the days in the year to pass over, why did she decide to leave us on my special day? I was certain it was more than coincidence.

In the days that followed, I spoke to Harry and he reassured me that Grandma was fine.

"*We celebrate when a child is born, and we celebrate when they return home,*" Harry explained.

"So you had a party in heaven?" I asked in disbelief, my imagination swimming with images of fiddlers, potato cakes, and men drinking porta.

Harry read my mind and chuckled. "*A little bit like your parties here,*" he answered with a smile. "*But all you need to concentrate on is that your Granny is safe and happy. I'm her brother and I'll look after her, alright? She's reunited with your Granddad John and she's where she's supposed to be. Nothing is your fault, alright?*"

I nodded slowly and felt a weight lift from my shoulders, but it didn't ease any of my concerns that there might be a reason she'd passed on my birthday. Every day, I constantly asked Harry *why*. Did Granny Kate pass over on my birthday for reasons that had yet to be explained? Did the timing of her death mean anything? Was it some sort of bad omen for me?

Finally, Harry looked me in the eyes sadly and gazed at me for a while. "*Bridget, I'm not sure whether I should be telling you this,*" he began. "*But to be sure, you're a bright girl, and you've worked some things out for yourself, that much I can see.*"

I waited for him to continue, my palms sweaty with anticipation. "*God works in mysterious ways,*" Harry said slowly. "*And there's usually a reason for everything, whether we can see it or not at the time. Your Granny Kate needed to leave you on your birthday to show you what bereavement is like.*"

I frowned, confused. "But why my birthday?" I asked. "I'd miss her any time of year!"

Harry nodded. "*Aye, but you thought about it more this way, didn't you?*" He pointed out gently. "*Leaving on your birthday gave you reason to wonder, a reason to develop.*"

I thought about this and it seemed to make sense. But what Harry said next made my hair stand up on end and my heart leap into my throat.

"*Bridget—your Granny Kate left on your birthday because you need to be prepared for a far greater loss: the loss of a person you love and depend on far, far more.*"

A few weeks after Grandma's death and Harry's message, I got the opportunity to spend some time alone with Dad. One of the cows was due to give birth and it was my turn to help with the delivery.

It was a hot, balmy summer night, and even at 3 a.m. the air inside the cowshed was still sticky and close. The cow had a hard birth and flailed around on the straw, grunting in pain as the calf got stuck on her way out.

I remember Dad tied a thick rope around the animal's tiny leg and we pulled her out by the light of the oil lamp, counting to three and heaving, over and over again, until our arms ached and the calf flopped on to the floor in a puddle of blood and mucus, her mother eating away at its birthing sack to welcome her baby to the world.

Every new animal on the farm was a wonder to me, and I never took these precious new lives for granted. I sat on a hay bale beaming from ear to ear, kicking my Wellington boots and watching the calf bleating her first breaths as her doting mother licked her clean and nuzzled the calf's head.

Dad grinned at me and tousled my hair playfully.

"Come on then, Bridget," he sighed. "We've stayed long enough, they're doing fine now. You'd better get some sleep before school."

I swung my legs down from the bale, wondering what we should call our new arrival, and joined Dad as he pushed the cowshed door open and held it for me.

The sky was as black as hell's kettle, but we didn't need Dad's oil lamp because it was ablaze with millions of stars, huge and sparkling like precious gems.

They were so breathtakingly beautiful I stopped walking, one hand clinging to Dad's arm and the other pointing up at the clear sky.

"Wow, Da. Look how many stars there are!" I exclaimed. "They look so near to us."

"Yes," Dad nodded, smiling into the twinkling blanket above.

"You see the small stars?" He said, pointing up at the sky. "Well, they represent the babies being born all over the world."

I looked at him, my eyes wide, and thought about the calf we'd just delivered.

"So there would be a new star in the sky tonight, Da?"

He looked down at my excited face and nodded, his eyebrows raised.

"Yes Bridget, that's it. And the bigger ones," he continued as I listened eagerly, "they represent people who've passed over to spirit."

I batted away a moth and scanned the diamond sky, locating a big star.

"It looks like it's moving," I murmured. "I wonder who that could be?"

"Well," Dad said slowly, "If you can find one star that is bigger or brighter than the others—one that stands out from the rest—that will be the star of someone you've known and loved."

I thought of Granny Kate and felt it was time to pass on my messages from spirit. I began by telling Dad that I'd questioned why Grandma had died on my birthday. He nodded and I took a breath.

"Harry said it was to teach me to be strong enough for the next person passing over," I told Dad in a small voice. "Someone much closer to me."

Dad put his arm around my shoulders and I hugged him back and told him it scared me. He seemed to know I had something else to say, but he was patient; we stood gazing at the beautiful sky in silence before I began.

"Harry told me when I'm twelve you're going to pass over to spirit," I said at last, in a shaky voice. "But I want you to stay with me forever."

Dad took my small hand and squeezed it tight in his rough grip. I expected him to reassure me; tell me not to be so silly. Instead, he looked me in the eyes and said, very calmly: "But that will be true. That will be true."

The breath caught in my throat and I stared into his eyes, searching for some sign he was playing with me, but there was no humour: only a grave sincerity as he gazed back at me. An owl hooted in the distance.

"I don't want to hear that," I wailed, my voice cracking. "Are you saying that in five years you're going to die?"

He nodded gently. "Yes."

I felt my legs turn to jelly as my mind struggled to accept this blow. I felt queasy and was lost for words, but Dad didn't seem to have any emotions there.

"I see exactly the same as you, Bridget," he explained softly. "Except I understand it better than you because I'm older. And when you're twelve, you'll be a very strong person and you will be ready."

Dad told me that even though the others would be older than me when it happened, I was special and would take over where he had left off. He explained that when he went, it wouldn't be goodbye: No, he wouldn't be here in person, but his spirit would be in heaven and he would always be with me to help and guide me through.

"I'll always be here to help you to deal with situations in your life, Bridget," he reassured me as tears streamed silently down my cheeks. "There's no need to be afraid."

The years passed, and although our conversation that night was always in the back of my mind, I tried to get on with my life as best I could. School, church, and the choir, Irish dancing, my chores on the farm.

Life was very basic but we were happy; I used to clean my teeth with my finger and a bowl of salt, because we didn't have anything else.

We couldn't have clothes all the time, so we took it in turns when money allowed, and when it was my turn I just got what was needed—one new pair of knickers, one pair of socks, a skirt, and a top for school, and these had to be best for everything.

Mum used to handwash all our clothes and dry them where she could. It must have been hard for her with so many of us, but as a child I loved watching the rows upon rows of washing on the line. We had a great wind up there and it was lovely watching them flutter in the breeze: waistcoats, Aran knitted jumpers, woolen skirts and stockings, English T-shirts sent by Kathleen, usually a size too big or small. I loved the fresh smell of the clothes when Mum brought them in.

I used to spend a lot of time in the hut where the chickens were kept. Quite often I'd pretend to be a teacher and imagine the chickens being pupils in my school; I'd teach them Gaelic and give them lessons on how important we were to each other. Our cats used to come into the hut when it was their time to give birth, so I was surrounded by nature, and that's when I felt happiest.

I'd spend hours on end waiting for the little chicks to hatch: they were like people to me. I called my two favourites Redhead and Strawberry and people would think I was mad, but I didn't care. I was never alone in the hut—my spirit friends would be there enjoying the games too.

My childhood was very rewarding; the only time I ever felt sad or upset was when I was thinking about Harry's prediction of my father's death.

However it was Great Aunt Bridget, who had first made me aware of the gift, who was next to pass. She died in the Castlebar home two years after my Granny Kate. Bridget was eighty-two by that time, and although she'd always spent a lot of time closed up in the bedroom and had been suffering from senile dementia for a few years now, I missed her presence in the house.

Around this time, Dad's health started to deteriorate. His arthritis became so acute that it almost crippled him, and I can recall him not being able to walk very well. His diabetes was also a worry—I didn't really understand his illness as a child, but I was glad that our golden retriever Sam could be with him on the cart when I was in school. Sometimes the only way we knew Dad had had a diabetes attack was when Sam came back to the cottage alone, barking and jumping up at us to sound the alarm, and would then take us to where Dad was lying ill.

My father never complained though, he would only ever slump into the kitchen chair next to the range and mumble that he had a headache. I began warming my hands on the fire and placing them on his temples to try and take the pain away, but Dad explained I didn't need to do that.

"You can do healing without warming your hands," he told me.

"Healing?"

"Just try it. Hold your hands on my head and just keep them there."

And so I did, placing my palms either side of his brow for quite some time, feeling my hands grow hotter and hotter, until Dad said the pain had gone.

One day Dad looked at me and said, "You will be the only one in this family that will be a fully qualified nurse. You'll go on to heal people and look after them, like you do with me."

Harry had told me on several occasions not only that I had healing hands, but also that I would be a nurse. He had also said there would come a time when I would have to choose between nursing and my gift.

I thought of these predictions as Dad spoke, and the images Harry had put in my mind of hospital uniforms. "Tell me more, Da!"

"In your later years you'll become a very well-known person," Dad continued. "People all over the world will reach out and touch your hands, but there will be other people guarding you."

I was puzzled. "Guarding me? Why?"

Dad took a breath as if wondering how best to explain.

"People will judge you, Bridget," he said at last. "And people will call you names; but you've always got to remember that everyone's entitled to their opinion. You'll be guarded so as not to get suffocated by people. So they can't invade your privacy."

My father made a lot of predictions, one of the most amazing ones when he was only a very young man. He was down in the peat bog with a friend from the village, a now elderly man whom I had the pleasure of meeting and hearing this story from only quite recently while I was back in Ireland to hold an audience at the Royal Theatre in Castlebar.

Dad had produced a matchbox from his jacket pocket and told his friend, "See this? In the future, people will be talking to each other all over the world using something this size." He grinned. "You mark my words."

His friend took little notice until some sixty years later when the mobile phone was finally invented.

Since Harry's terrible message after Granny Kate's passing, I made it a priority to spend every minute of my spare time with Dad. We were inseparable. Quite often we'd be down at the peat bog digging, and I'd shout *watch out!* because there was something coming towards us. But Dad, knowing it was only spirit, would reassure me. "It's just passing, Bridget," he would smile knowingly. "Just passing."

I would often accompany Dad on the cart, the donkey pulling in front, as we'd head off to the little village of Ballyvary.

In the small square stood a butcher's, doctor's, and the post office. There were terraced houses, the only two-storey buildings in our area, and the Garda station. There was a petrol pump, Stinson's and Canning's pubs, and three shops: Eva Gerraghty's, Frank O'Reilly's, and Ann Maloney's.

I always went to these shops with Dad and we seemed to spend an entire day doing nothing. Dad would talk to the shopkeepers while I'd look around at the goods piled up on the wooden shelves: food for people, birds and animals, spades and farm tools of all kinds, tobacco and snuff and clay pipes, custard powder and marmalade. There were needles and thread, buttons and thimbles, sugar and salt, mouth organs and tin whistles, oil lamps and cans, stout and whisky, cornflour and tea. Starch, sweets and chocolate, jam, mustard seeds, brylcreem, castor oil, ginger beer, rice-meal, razor blades, bicycle tyres, barley, knives, candles, and wax polish. You name it, you could get it in Ballyvary.

One day when we came out of one particular shop and got up on the cart, the donkey set off in the wrong direction and took us up into the yard of a farm that wasn't ours. When Dad caught the lads who had swapped their donkey for ours he was none too pleased, but we still laughed about it all the way home!

CHAPTER

4

My twelfth birthday arrived on the 8th June 1968. Harry's prediction (and Dad's confirmation of this) five years earlier was pushed to the back of my mind, and life continued as normal. That is, until the following October, when a chance comment he made on one such trip to the village finally prepared me for what was to come.

We had taken the donkey and cart down to Ballyvary and were in Ann Maloney's shop. Dad used to call into Canning's, the pub next door, while I would help Mrs. Maloney with the washing, or go down to the well for her to collect water.

When Dad had drank a couple of whiskys and talked with the men in the village, he would meet me back in the shop and we'd stock up on groceries before setting off back home. Women and children were never seen in a pub!

My eldest brothers and sister had by this time crossed the water to England, and it was a custom of Dad's that a Christmas box would be sent to each of them to help them with dinner. Usually, money wouldn't stretch too far, so really it was only a goose or turkey we sent, no trimmings.

This particular day I was just sitting in the back room as I often did: listening to the wireless, tidying up, and helping Mrs. Maloney with her chores.

Dad had just returned from the pub and Mrs. Maloney's conversation turned to the parcels. In those days the hampers would take anything up to a week to get to England, so it all had to be carefully planned months in advance.

"Do you want to start sorting out the Christmas boxes, Charlie?" Mrs. Maloney asked cheerfully. "It's about time we got them organised."

"No. I won't be needing them this year, Ann," Dad replied matter-of-factly.

My ears pricked up and I sneaked toward the door separating the rooms and peered around the frame. I saw the confused expression on Mrs. Maloney's face.

"Why ever not?" She frowned.

"Well, all the family will be together for Christmas this year," Dad replied, choosing his words carefully.

Mrs. Maloney looked at him for a while and fidgeted with the beads around her neck. Then, quietly, she asked:

"What are you trying to say, Charlie?"

Dad smiled and replied calmly, "I won't be here at Christmas. I'll be in heaven looking down on all of them."

I heard every word of it, plain as day, and I waited until we got back into the cart before confronting him. Normally I sat at the back of the trap so it was level, but that day I joined Dad at the front. My quivering bottom lip and pale face must have given away what I had heard, but Dad said nothing: we had plenty of time to discuss it on the ride back to the farm.

"Da," I began, swallowing hard. "Why did you say that to Mrs. Maloney?"

Dad held the reins and stared ahead as the donkey trotted off. He took a long time to speak and every second was an eternity—I was terrified of his reply; I willed him to tell me he was simply having a joke with her.

"Bridget, you know what Harry told you," Dad finally answered, looking at me with pity in his eyes. He sighed. "We've spoken about this before; I told you when the time comes you will be strong."

I began to cry, and Dad took one hand from the reins to put his arm around my shoulders as I sobbed.

"But I was twelve back in June and you didn't die," I protested. "Harry got it wrong." The tears blurred my vision and I buried my head into his jacket, which smelled of the carbolic soap he shaved with every day.

Dad's grip around me tightened; I sensed his sadness on my behalf as I shook with fear and grief, the sobs racking my body.

"Yes, you were twelve in June, Bridget," He said gently. "And you'll still be twelve at Christmas when I go."

I had never disbelieved anything Dad had told me before, but this was a turning point: I felt helpless, like a rabbit caught in one of our snares. Harry's prediction was unfolding right in front of my eyes and I was powerless to stop it.

From that point I tended to spend a lot more time in my own head and talking to spirit, working out how I would cope when the time came for Dad to die. Where was he going to be when he passed? Who would find him? How would things carry on from there? I wanted so badly to share my fear, to have someone comfort me and cry with me. But the only person I felt able to do this with was Dad, and he was the one who had broken the news: I had no choice but to deal with it alone.

Dad's worsening diabetes forced him to be hospitalized for thirteen weeks, shortly after our trip to Mrs. Maloney's shop. It's strange: I have no recollection of this, only vague, fragmented memories of all the times I was on the land without him and how alone I felt. On the 17th December though, he seemed to have stabilised and the hospital told us he was due to come home at last.

In those days nobody had a telephone and we all used the one at Doherty's shop. My mother, in high spirits at the news, had allowed me to stay off school and asked me to run and call the hospital to see what time Dad would be ready to come home.

I set off around 9:30 a.m. on that cold winter morning, taking a short cut through the fields. The excitement of my father coming home made my insides smile. I felt I would burst if I tried to contain the sensation, so when it tingled through my body and made its exit through my limbs I was off and away, running and skipping and jumping through the high grass just to let it out.

When I reached the church, out of breath and still delirious with excitement, I looked up and noticed an enormous star above the steeple. Our neighbour, Maggie McDonald, was coming in the opposite direction.

I never saw Maggie in anything other than big hair rollers and a *plaikeen* scarf around her head. She used to secretly smoke and drink and would give us money to bring her woodbines and black *porta* behind her husband's back; we'd get a penny for our troubles. We would put the liquor and tobacco in a hiding place for her to collect, like a hole in a dry stone wall, and as far as I know her husband was none the wiser.

This particular day, I stopped running as Maggie approached me, and I pointed out the star to her. "Won't you look at that star," I panted. "Isn't it strange?"

"Star?" Maggie squinted into the sky where I had gestured. After a few moments, she turned back to me. "But there *is* no star, Bridget O'Malley."

Maggie McDonald weighed me up with narrowed eyes, curious and wary in equal measure. "Now I know what Charlie meant when he said you were special."

I didn't have time to wonder about this comment; I'd had a sudden flash of realisation that knocked the breath out of me: the night when I was birthing the calf with Dad, the night we'd seen the star that represented my grandmother's passing. Could *this* star … ? I felt sick finishing the thought.

My excitement fell away like a snake shedding its skin, and underneath it was revealed another, truer emotion:

fear. My heart caught in my throat; had I been blinded by my initial happiness? Was this star my preparation, my warning?

It's funny how gut feelings have a lot in common with joy: both give you butterflies. Both are waiting for something to happen. I didn't know which feeling to trust.

The sky mirrored my confusion. It looked like it understood, like it too was the product of an internal battle. Dull and grey, yet bright somehow. A comforting stillness in the air high above the steeple, contrasted with the blustery winds bending the saplings and kicking up the grass angrily at ground level, as if in warning for the worst kind of outcome.

The bad feeling gnawed at my excitement, growing until there was hardly any joy in me, just a knotted ball of apprehension and nerves. I tried to push my intuition aside and concentrate on the fact we'd been told by the doctors Dad *was* coming home, but you can't easily ignore a gut feeling. It doesn't stop, nagging you while you think of positive thoughts, entering your happiness like an unwelcome guest.

The nagging got louder and louder until it became a riot of screeching knowledge inside me. Dad wasn't coming home. Dad wasn't coming home. I sprinted to Doherty's, praying all the while that for once in my life, my intuition was wrong. But it wasn't.

Dad was in a coma and wouldn't be coming home, the nurse on the other end told me. "You are all to come to Castlebar hospital immediately," she advised gently.

It hit me like a freight train. I felt the force of the news crash into me almost physically, knocking me off my balance and scattering my thoughts like a bowling ball knocking down pins. Only one thought remained, overwhelming and dark and inescapable: This is it. This is it.

There was no shock. Only the bland, quiet reality of what the nurse had told me. What Harry had told me. What my father had softly confirmed.

After somehow managing to send telegrams to my siblings across the water, I came out of Doherty's shop, alone and in shock, and back on to the road feeling numb. How would I break the news to my family, waiting for me back at the farm?

A mist had descended over the church steeple as if it was a metaphor for my spirit, and the star had disappeared. Disappeared, along with my daydreams of Dad coming home: his big, rough hands tousling my hair in greeting, his strong arms scraping me up for a bear hug, his hearty laugh filling our cottage once again as we celebrated his good health.

I ran in blind panic across the fields, cutting my leg badly on some barbed wire as I clambered over a wall. I remember seeing the blood, sticky against my brown skirt and warm as it trickled down my ankle socks onto my shoes; but I felt no physical pain. Only my insides were hurting.

On hearing the message of my father's imminent death, Mum's legs buckled and she collapsed with the shock. When she had regained her composure, she hauled herself up and changed into her Sunday best—a pretty cream dress with pink roses, with a peach-coloured cardigan and flat sandals on her feet. She looked graceful and beautiful, and very young.

Too young to be saying goodbye to the only love of her life.

At the hospital, two nurses were chatting in the corridor as if this was a perfectly normal day, whilst a porter bustled by pushing an elderly man in a wheelchair. The air was thick with the smell of disinfectant and sickness, and I had to fight hard to stop the panic rising as we hurried in silence to Dad's ward.

He had been there for three months at that point, so we were frequent visitors and had become accustomed to the hospital. Usually, we could see his bed from the entrance, but that day it had been moved near to the door and the curtains had been pulled around him. I remember wondering whether they only did that if it was bad news, and I could hear the blood rushing around in my head as my heart pounded.

A male nurse called Kevin met us in the ward. He had mousy blonde hair parted to one side and wore a white coat over his tall frame. His kind eyes twinkled as he greeted us, betraying the grave expression on his face.

Kevin led us to Dad's bedside and the curtains were pulled back to reveal him looking grey and old, weaker than I'd ever seen him. He had a drip in his arm and a tube in his nose, with a bag at the side of his bed collecting his urine.

I will never forget those scenes and the overwhelming feeling of helplessness they caused me; his eyelids flickering and his breathing slow and ragged as his lungs struggled to keep going.

Kevin explained gently that Dad's coma meant he could hear us but couldn't respond, and I could sense the sadness he had for our family as he explained it was unlikely Dad would pull through. Mum listened to the news, choked back a sob, then collected herself, taking a bottle of holy water from her pocket with shaking hands.

She anointed my father, making a cross on his forehead and placing some holy water in his mouth. He didn't react. She said the rosary with a small but determined voice, as the rest of us looked at the floor and were quiet in our own thoughts. The look on her face was enough to tell us that the end was near, and Billy started crying, a small, wailing noise that echoed everyone's emotions.

Mum squeezed Dad's twitching fingers and I heard her whisper something to him—I couldn't hear the words, but I knew she had bravely accepted his fate and was saying goodbye from all of us.

The priest arrived to give Dad the last rites and I remember wanting to shake him and shout that Dad wasn't going anywhere; he wasn't needed here. I wanted to be with Dad on my own. I wanted to hug him and beg him to stay with us; to tell him I wasn't ready for him to leave, and I hated seeing my mother so desperate in her grief.

Then Kevin stepped forward, lifting Dad's frail head up very slowly and using his index finger and thumb to open Dad's eyes. In contrast with his pale skin, they were as bright blue and alive as I'd ever seen them, and I took some comfort from that.

Kevin said, "Charles, your wife and five of your nine children are here." He asked us all our names and then told Dad who was there with him. I felt that Dad tried to say something but couldn't, and a deep sadness washed over me.

The fate of my father, a fate I had known for five years, was now staring at me, unblinking, unwavering, not about to change its mind. There was nothing left to argue with, nothing else to turn my thoughts to, no hope to throw in front of this monstrous fact: This is it. The prediction. This is it.

As Kevin laid his head gently back down, a beautiful smile spread across Dad's face. It seemed to say, *"don't be sad. I'm going to a better place."* It occurred to me then that it was selfish of me to want him to stay; to expect him to put up with all the pain he'd had for such a long time. Dad was waiting until we'd said farewell so he could let go of it all and make a peaceful journey to the afterlife.

Emotions ran through me at such speed it all became too much: insecurity, the gaping hole in our father-daughter bond that was impossible to fill. Intense sadness, like falling into a pit so deep you can't see any light and there is only the blackness of despair. A burning anger that rose in my chest as I recalled my premature excitement at his homecoming only that morning. But there was pride, too: a deep sense of respect and gratitude that this wonderful man was my father.

When we came out of the hospital to get into the taxi, I went to speak and found that I had completely lost my voice. I couldn't make a sound. Even so, I was determined to take over where my father had left off and be strong for my mother—as soon as we got home I took a notepad and pencil and went to see her cousins, John and Kate Knight.

I must have looked a sight as I stood in their house trying desperately to get the words out. They waited with growing concern as I struggled to form a sentence, eventually scribbling down that horrible day's events in my notepad. Of course they came at once, but there was absolutely nothing they could do to console my mother. She was losing the man that she had loved all her life.

The day went by as best it could, considering. Mum tried to make something to eat and do the washing and cleaning, but the chores seemed trivial in view of the grief that hung over the house like a suffocating blanket.

Everything was grey and dismal. The atmosphere was heavy with the weight of our impending loss, and an eerie silence filled the cottage. No one spoke, not even my mother, and that is how the rest of the day passed. Each of us dealing with the shock individually, knowing that words were futile.

CHAPTER

5

Dad passed over that night: Tuesday 17th December 1968 at 8.45 p.m. I was twelve years old and the prediction had come to pass.

It was pitch black and there was a knock on the door at quarter past nine at night. It was my father's brother Pat. I can only assume that Doherty's had received a phone call from the hospital and the message was passed on that way.

Pat had come back up the road to tell us, and I will never forget him walking through the door of our cottage. He was wearing a flat cap, a beige waistcoat, jacket and trousers. It was the first time I ever looked at him and marveled at how much he resembled my father; I'd never noticed that before.

Pat gave us the news, cloth cap in hand, and everyone broke down in tears. But the strangest thing happened to me. I didn't cry but instead became hysterical with laughter. I'd got the giggles to the point where I couldn't stop: even after Mum slapped me hard across the face I was still uncontrollable.

I knew in my own head that I shouldn't have been laughing; that it wasn't a normal reaction to my father's death. But I just couldn't stop and my sides were aching. The feeling was unreal. My mind was whirling and minutes later when the laughter had subsided, all I kept thinking was, you knew about this. You expected it. How does it feel *now?*

I left the room and wandered into my brothers' room. It was pitch black, but the curtains were open and there was light shining in from the moonlit sky. I stood looking out of the window, feeling numb and allowing the news to sink in.

Suddenly I saw the star I'd seen earlier above the church. This time it was moving: It shot across the sky and came to a halt over our garden.

Right in the centre of that star I saw my father, as plain as day. He was wearing the green striped pyjamas he'd been in that morning, along with a lovely smile and a full head of beautiful brown hair. He waved to me, and then the star took him back up. I have never seen a star as big or bright since that night.

I knew then that, just as he'd told me years before, he was always going to be with me and everything would be all right. And strangely enough, just as he had told me I would be, I was strong. I never shed a tear. I felt it was my duty to see to everybody and make sure Mum was looked after; I didn't feel I had the right to grieve because I was warned about it.

But at the same time, he was my dad. He was my world.

In just a few years we had lost both my grandparents, my Great Aunt Bridget, and now my father. The cottage felt cold and empty for the first time ever, as if it had emotions of its own and knew something of our despair. I was exhausted but the thought of going to bed was unbearable: I knew it was only the first of many long, lonely nights Dad wouldn't be there to tuck us in and light the oil lamp.

I fell out with God. I refused to pray the night Dad passed; I wanted to scream with anger at God's decision, I wanted justification as to why he had taken the head of our family so close to Christmas. My faith was replaced with a sense of abandonment and my emotions bubbled through me once again. I was seething with anger and sadness, anxiety and frustration, apprehension and loneliness.

I sneaked a glass of whisky to help me nod off, it burned my throat and did nothing to drown my sorrows but it felt good getting some small revenge by sinning.

When I eventually lay down on the bed to go to sleep, I hoped desperately that Harry would visit me and bring along my father. But I couldn't feel any spirit presence that night; the grief made it impossible. I began to wonder whether Harry's business with me was finished, that once the prophecy was fulfilled it was the end of a chapter and my gift would die with my father's memory.

As if in response to my thoughts, Harry's previous messages swam through my mind, and although in my despair I couldn't see or hear him, I sensed he tried to comfort me: "*We did prepare you, right from the minute you started speaking to us when you were three years old, and at your grandmother's death on your birthday. We told you there was something bigger to come. So if you sit and let us talk to you, we will see you through this as well.*"

My siblings in England arrived the day after Dad's passing. There was a strange atmosphere on their arrival: a mix of happiness that we were all finally together again, but sadness at the circumstances in which we were reunited. The house was busier, warmer, noisier—*normal*, once again—but Dad's absence had caused a gaping wound in the family, and their arrival only seemed to make it more obvious and more painful.

We all spent the night of the eighteenth together, with Kathleen and Mum discussing the funeral arrangements. I sat in contemplation as they spoke, remembering all the times my brothers and sister had visited us, and how very sad my father was for days on end after they'd returned to England.

Perhaps what made Dad's passing worse was that three grandchildren had been born that very summer: Peter to Charles; David to Fergie; and Katherine, Kathleen's fourth baby. Dad had never met these new members of his family, and it seemed such a huge shame that my nephews and niece would grow up not knowing what a wonderful man their grandfather was.

There were three full days of celebration before my father was buried, with people from the village collecting at the house for the wake, bringing whisky and porta and offering their condolences, as they had for Granny Kate.

They came at all hours of the day, shaking their heads and saying, "I'm so sorry for your trouble," discussing Dad and what he meant to them, telling anecdotes and sharing memories.

I recall thinking it's amazing how well you're thought about when you've passed over. I was angry at their kind words because I knew even as a child that Dad probably had quite a few more enemies than friends: he was well known for opening his mouth and putting things in place. He was always very direct in what he said and thought, and he stood up for himself. It's a pity those people didn't have nice things to say while he was alive, and I sensed that not all of them were well meaning.

On the second day of the wake my suspicions were proven when I got my voice back after a good twenty-four hours of being mute. I'd noticed a neighbour of ours rummaging through Mum's bag and looking very shifty. I knew something wasn't right and a high-pitched shout erupted from my lungs and alerted my brothers: John knocked seven bells of hell out of the fella and threw him out of the house.

There wasn't a big fuss about it and I don't remember it ever being discussed afterwards; my family didn't want anyone to know that somebody could be so disgusting as to steal the money we needed for Dad's funeral.

Those first few days and nights passed in a blur while neighbours and family continued to come in droves to pay their respects.

It was a bitter, frosty December and our bedroom felt ice cold—even with the open fire crackling, its golden flames licking the shadows on the stone hearth. I huddled up against Rose, Peter, and Oliver close in bed, shivering into the blankets. Our bedroom had never felt so cold and empty.

I sensed Harry's presence very strongly at the bottom of my bed. I knew he was trying to make contact but I blocked him out; I was desperate to hear any news of Dad but I was still very angry with Harry—and terrified of him giving me any more predictions of death.

On the morning of the nineteenth, we all rose early to the noise of pans and kettles clanging in the kitchen: the sound of Mum making breakfast as best she could. We ate gruel and soda bread with butter; I remember we had jam that day too, which was usually a rare treat. Mum heated some water on the stove and we took it in turns to strip wash.

That evening we went to the Chapel of Rest at Castlebar County Hospital to say our final goodbyes to Dad.

Mum didn't want to upset us any more than was necessary, so she had made the decision not to bring Dad's body home: the normal thing to do in a Catholic household. She did the right thing as far as I was concerned, because it would have been the first time in my life that Dad was there with me and unable to answer my questions.

In death, Dad's skin was strangely transparent; so pale without the blood in his cheeks. As a farmer he'd always had a ruddy complexion, the elements weathering his face over the years and making him look real and alive.

Now, it had lost every trace of colour, and was milk-white and as delicate as a paper mask. He didn't look like the strong, solid man I had known. His skin was waxy and his expression was stiff and set, like his face had been carved from an altar candle. There was dried blood on his chin where he had been shaved and prepared for his casket.

Like Granny Kate, Dad was wearing the habit used to dress the dead; it was a horrible brown colour and I remember thinking how it didn't suit him.

We said goodbye in turn, my mother first. She wrapped rosary beads tenderly around his hand, and weeping silently, she whispered to her husband that God willing, she would see him again in a better place.

Kathleen broke down as she approached the coffin, sobbing uncontrollably and kissing Dad's forehead, her tears falling on his habit. The others kept their goodbyes quiet and dignified, all except Billy, who found the farewell too much and fled from the chapel before it was his turn.

I simply stood and looked at my father for as long as I was able to. I placed his hand in mine: it was like holding cold metal. I wanted to kiss his face but couldn't, because I was so used to my kisses touching warm skin.

Any minute now, he's going to open his eyes and say this is all a big practical joke, I pleaded over and over. I could see a beautiful smile etched into the waxy face. It grew bigger and wider by the second; I couldn't tell whether it was my imagination or not.

At 8:30 p.m. we took Dad's coffin to St. Peter and Paul's church in Straide, ready for mass the following morning. I remember Mum's brave face as we arrived home nearing midnight, trying to sort out the little ones and juggle our bedtime routine with her own grief. She explained gently that Dad was in heaven and we needed to get some sleep for his burial the next day.

Dad had a joint funeral with Mary Howley, another lady from Straide, and the throngs of mourners were shaking hands with us down the line. My family occupied the first two pews in church and Dad's coffin was on the left, its lid now closed forever. The silence in church was stifling, peppered with the occasional sniffle and sob. All I could think during the sermon was "*Is he alright in there?*"

I wondered about who would greet him in the afterlife: were his sisters still alive in America, or would they be there to guide him over? What about Granny Kate and Granddad John, or his own parents? Perhaps he was with Great Aunt Bridget, or even my Uncle Harry—who I wasn't ready to hear from just yet.

These daydreams kept me sane and brought me some comfort as the mass came to an end and my brothers carried Dad's coffin once more on the long walk from the church to the graveyard. They seemed dignified in their grief, their heads held high as they walked to his final resting place.

Dad was buried on a hill with a beautiful view of the valley below. He had always said that a gravestone is simply a place to visit, to commemorate a life on earth: nothing more, nothing less. But nevertheless, I am grateful that the sun will always shine down on him in that spot.

"*Ashes to ashes, dust to dust,*" the priest spoke solemnly. "*May the Lord have mercy on your soul, and the souls of all the faithful departed.*"

"*Amen,*" came the murmured response.

But Mum was wailing and screaming like a banshee; terrible cries of grief that sent shivers down my spine. Her pain was raw and it overwhelmed everyone gathered around. Peter and Oliver cried their little hearts out, Billy was sobbing uncontrollably, and the elder ones wept quietly.

Hot tears streamed down my cheeks as my mind whirled with questions and my sobs caught in my throat. Why did Harry choose me? Why hadn't I seen or heard from him or Dad since? Was this it? Would my gift die with Dad? It was as though none of my experiences made sense any more, and I questioned my faith in eternal life. Would I ever be shown more proof, or was this it? Was my father destined to rot in this hole forever?

In my grief and confusion, it took me a long time to realise Dad was right: he wasn't in that ground at all; it was just his shell. But walking away and watching the gravediggers fill in the deep pit, I couldn't help breaking down at the thought of his body in that box, the soil flying from the spades and hitting its lid, the horrendous realisation that, in this life at least, I would never see my father again.

Dad's clothes were buried where I had seen his star— under the vegetable patch in the garden, as was the tradition. But I remember feeling that the farm meant nothing to me anymore, and I suppose Mum must have felt the same because on the night of Dad's funeral, she sat us down and explained that we were leaving our homeland for good. Our things were packed up, neighbours came to collect the cattle from our fields, and by the twenty-third of December 1968 we were travelling to Dublin to board a plane heading for England.

❀ PART TWO ❀
My Gift
Through
Love and
Loss

CHAPTER 6

If I could have my time back again, it would be those wonderful years in Ireland I'd choose to re-live. I've never been as happy as I was between the ages of seven to twelve, and I found it very hard leaving my birthplace. Everything had changed; my life was turned upside down.

At only twenty-four, and grieving for a father she loved dearly, Kathleen already had four children and a husband to think of, and now had to put up with Rose, Billy, Mum, and I living with her too. I sensed that married life wasn't easy for her and I felt guilty for intruding.

Peter and Oliver were living with Charlie and his wife, Anne. She became their surrogate mother during that turbulent time, bringing them up along with her own baby (also called Peter) who was born that year.

Once a week we all went to eat at my brother Fergie and his wife Pam's house. Looking back, it's amazing they had time to even give us a meal—their son David, just five months old, was very poorly and had recently had major heart surgery. Everything was absolutely chaotic.

We had no space or time to grieve for Dad. Rose was silent and withdrawn, Billy was his usual emotional self and Mum was still in shock; she seemed oblivious to everything. On our arrival in England, the only thing she wanted to know was the location of the nearest church. It was left to Kathleen to find us a family doctor and sort out all the arrangements for school.

I dealt with things by keeping busy, and tried to make myself useful by doing chores: washing nappies or going to the launderette for Kathleen. Everything was totally alien. I remember being fascinated by simple technologies such as the washing machine and light switches, being able to run a hot bath or watch television.

The downside of my new life was that there was too much time to think. In Ireland we never had a minute to ourselves, what with the chores, animals, and long walk to school, and of course the spirit friends I played with while I was working on the farm or going about my busy day. At Kathleen's I had no comfort, and the abundance of modern conveniences meant that there were always a couple of hours in each day where I had nothing to do but dwell on what had happened, and how sad I was feeling.

The sky at night was the most disappointing thing about England. It didn't seem to be as black as my Irish sky, and it didn't have as many stars. I used to stand outside for hours in the garden, hoping to see my father's star and wondering whether my spirit friends would follow me over the water.

Then, as I'd hoped, Dad came to me on Christmas Day.

Although the family was separated for lunch—all in our respective new homes—we did see each other for the rest of the day at Kathleen's, and it was only John who had stayed behind in Ireland.

After attending church, the whole family bustled around downstairs: basting the turkey, preparing the vegetables, and listening to carols on the wireless. After my chores, I went to sit alone in my room and contemplate our first Christmas without my dear father.

Suddenly, the energy in the room shifted, a sure sign I wasn't alone. I spun around on my bed to see my father standing in the room, smiling at me. He wasn't wearing his glasses, and his tweed farm clothing had been replaced by a black suit—as though he'd been to a funeral. I'm still not sure why that was; I was so bowled over I forgot to ask him.

"*Now you listen to me,*" his voice came in my head, soft and stern all at once. "*You just try to enjoy today. No crying. I'm here with you all and I will be here whenever you need me.*"

I blinked back tears and nodded slowly, my anger fading to a deep sense of comfort at his presence. My head was swimming with questions. At that point I still didn't understand my gift fully, and I remember wondering how on earth Dad had found us all in England.

I regained my composure and we spoke for about twenty minutes. It was wonderful. He told me once again that I had to be strong, that I was special and that it was me who would have to help him take care of the family.

"*I know it's hard, Bridget, but I promised you that as you got older you'd understand. Rose and your mother need you,*" Dad told me.

Rose hadn't said a word about Dad since he passed, and as far as I am aware hasn't spoken of it to this day. It seemed to hit her hardest of all.

Dad confided in me that Mum had lost two other children, a boy and a girl, in addition to Charles's twin.

"*They're here with me,*" he said. "*It's grand where I am, Bridget, and I want no more sadness from you. You just call me and I'll be here. Things will get easier and you'll be happy. Start with today.*"

I told Dad I had fallen out with God, and he told me sternly that I hadn't to think like that. "*God does exist, Bridget. I will always be here to help you through these obstacles—just be strong.*"

It was just what I'd expected Dad to say, and I felt comforted: if Dad wasn't angry about being taken, I should find it in my heart to forgive God. I was a Catholic—believing in the Almighty was a crucial part of who I was. I opened my mouth to tell Dad I would try to be grown-up and mature about things, but our conversation was interrupted when I was called down for Christmas dinner.

It was, as expected, a sombre occasion, which I tried my best to get through without bursting into tears. I remember the tension, everyone feeling the same sense of emptiness at Dad's absence—and Kathleen seemed extremely stressed—but we all ploughed on and tried to pretend we were having a good time regardless of the gloomy atmosphere in the room.

Later, I told Mum about Dad's visit. She looked at me in silence as I spoke, as if weighing me up. I'm not sure she believed me until I mentioned the two babies she had miscarried, at which point something in her eyes changed and she nodded, her gaze shifting to the floor.

"Yes," she muttered.

No more was said on the matter, but I could feel Dad's presence while we spoke and was sure she often felt it too. Of course, Mum's reaction to my words was a major moment for me as a grieving child. There was a glimmer of hope now that I might one day be able to say more, to give her messages regularly, to be open about my gift. But I didn't feel it was the right time to press her, and decided instead to let Mum think about the implications in her own time—she could always broach the subject with me when she felt ready, I thought.

Despite Dad's visit and my knowledge that he would always be there, the sense of sadness I had continued and I was still finding his absence hard to deal with.

After a few weeks of struggling to get through each day, I heard Harry telling me: "*Soldier on, soldier on.*"

Like a light switch being turned on, I suddenly realised my gift was priceless. I had something nobody else had, and I should always be grateful that I had the help of spirit in such a difficult time. I started to feel that if I lost Harry I would lose my connection to Ireland. So I made a pact with myself: the daytime was for learning, and the evenings were for communicating with spirit. I would go home, do my chores and homework, and then spend half an hour talking to spirit—Dad, Harry, Granny Kate, and Great Aunt Bridget.

I started to feel Grandma around me for the first time, and Bridget came back to me several times while living at Kathleen's. I think they knew I needed them more than ever.

Most of the time I simply heard their voices, speaking as clearly as anyone else in the room. They'd have conversations between themselves, everyone chipping in, and I remember as a child forgetting to answer telepathically and speaking out loud to them—which confused and infuriated my family because I was never listening to what was happening in this world!

Sometimes the visits were on the physical plane: Bridget and Granny Kate came back looking like identical twins, their berets gone, their hair long and grey and peppered with mousy brown streaks. I spoke to each one individually, but naturally it was always Dad I wanted to communicate with the most.

We spoke of Mum—how brave she was, how she needed my help, but that I was right not to force my gift on her, of my siblings and my life, and how I shouldn't be frightened to be who I was.

I started to develop my gift more and more; I could feel myself opening up to it. The spirit visitations happened every night and they got me through that year, the toughest of my life so far.

I started at Eastfield secondary school in Lightcliffe, West Yorkshire, after Christmas.

It was a big transition for me, moving from my small Irish village school with around 190 children to a huge, foreboding place with nearly two thousand pupils. Peter and Oliver went to a different school and Rose and Billy had finished their education, so I was completely alone. For the first time in my life I saw children of other classes and races, and I felt as if they were looking at me.

I found it very hard; even the lessons were different and I'd gone from a class of twelve to a rowdy class of thirty. In Ireland we learned Irish, English, Maths, History, and Geography—but at Eastfield, in addition to those subjects we had French, German, Home Economics, and P.E. too—and in Religious Education we learned about all the world's religions, which was very strange for a Catholic child brought up to believe there was only one God and one way of praising him!

My gift helped me get through all the overwhelming changes. If I were ever feeling down or panicky, I would hear Dad saying, "*You'll have to sink or swim, Bridget.*"

To my surprise and relief, my Irish spirit friends began to visit me in the classroom. Lucy in particular appeared regularly, causing mischief by pulling faces behind the teacher's back, sticking her tongue out or tugging at her ears as we were reading aloud in class, and pretending to tickle pupils who obviously couldn't see her. I was always in trouble for fidgeting or giggling to myself, but I found it comforting that I wasn't alone, and my questions about whether spirit can travel had been answered.

I knew I needed to make an effort to fit in, and luckily my thick Irish accent made me quite a novelty! Everyone wanted to know all about me, and before long I had made new friends.

I was closest to Lynn Walker, Linda Thornton, and Susan Oade. As time went on I confided in them about the fairies, banshees, leprechauns, and spirit children, and they found it fascinating. Nobody disputed this, they just asked a lot of questions, so I felt able to tell them about my connections on the other side.

I was surprised to learn that a lot of my school friends had suffered grief too. Several of them had lost friends or grandparents, and knowing this took away some of the loneliness I felt at losing Dad. It was also strange to me, coming from a Catholic village, that many of my classmates had no father living at home. The idea of divorce made me feel lucky: at least I still had a family unit, and could speak to Dad whenever I wanted.

I enjoyed every aspect of school, especially wearing a uniform (we didn't have these in Ireland), but the most important thing to me was my school lunch. Money at home was so tight it was the only meal I would have that day. There were so many delicious English meals that were new to me: sponge pudding with treacle, toad in the hole (sausages baked in batter), chicken curry, breaded fishfingers, beef burgers, battered cod and fried chipped potatoes, cottage pie (minced beef and vegetables with a mashed potato topping), and Yorkshire puddings filled with gravy—few English people would eat a traditional Sunday roast without those! The dinner lady always gave me more than everyone else and I had seconds on top; I think she knew my situation and took pity on me.

These were the most unhappy times of my life, and school became a haven, a welcome respite from the misery I continued to feel inside.

This situation went on for what seemed like forever, but in January 1969 I was relieved and excited to learn we were returning to my beloved homeland for a holiday.

Mum, myself, Billy, and Oliver went back to Straide for about six months. It must have been the time Mum was finalising the sale of the farm, but she never discussed her business with us and we were expected not to ask any questions.

I know that during this trip we stayed in our cottage, but I don't have any memories of the family home after Dad died. I think I've chosen not to recall it; the farm meant nothing to me without him.

Mum sold the house to a couple, but they later separated and the house stood unoccupied. Due to Irish laws, the council took over the farm. I'm not sure what happened to our land, but the cottage itself stands empty even today.

One night just after we returned to Straide, Mum took my brothers to visit a family friend while I went with my cousin Mary Knight up the big hill to Jimmy Lavelle's. Jimmy was a lovely old gentleman, and like Harry, he walked with a limp and had never married.

The card nights he held at his little thatched cottage were well known in the village, and on any given night the men would gather to drink whisky and porta and play games through the night. As kids we never joined in, but we were all made welcome and were allowed to watch. We'd collect there because if any of us were courting it would be the only time that you could see each other without your parents' knowledge!

This particular night, it was pitch black walking up to his house, and Mary and I were linking arms tightly. After living in England for a month and getting used to the light pollution I felt scared going up the road, although the moon was shining as brightly as usual.

As we were passing the Stinson's farm, I heard a bull thudding down the field toward us, its hooves pounding the earth, the snorting of its nostrils as it drew nearer. I froze in fear before hearing an almighty thud as the bull smashed into a tree at the bottom of the field. I found my voice and gripped Mary even harder.

"Oh my God," I gasped, petrified.

"What?" Mary asked, pulling at my arm to keep walking.

"Didn't you hear that bull, how he was coming at us?" I squealed.

"What are you talking about?" Mary replied. "There are no cattle in that field."

"Yes there are! Didn't you hear that bull running at us?"

Mary was adamant there were no bulls in the field and we squabbled about it all the way to Jimmy's. I was sure I'd be proved right, but the men gathered with their glasses and cards confirmed that not only were there no cattle in that field, but none grazing anywhere nearby. I eventually let my confusion go and we settled into the night.

Possibly an hour later, we saw car headlights coming up the road. I assumed it was my Mum coming for me, and I stood up to say my goodbyes.

When the car turned in to the drive, I saw that it was Jimmy Doherty, the taxi driver who had taken us to Dublin airport after Dad's death. My first thought was that something terrible had happened to Mum and my brothers, but Jimmy was looking for Jack—a man who was in the house playing cards.

He explained he had very bad news and took Jack out into the yard to tell him that his brother had been killed that night. It was a terrible crash: a lorry had run straight into him knocking him off his bicycle on the road from Foxford. I looked at my cousin with my heart racing. The accident happened at exactly the same time as I heard the bull crash into the tree at the Stinson's farm.

CHAPTER 7

On our return to England I felt in turmoil. The prospect of leaving Straide for a second time was terrible, and on top of that I had missed six months of school.

I asked Mum to stay, begged her to return for good, but she told me that she and my father had made a pact: the whole family would stay together in one place after his death.

Since Kathleen, Charlie, and Fergie had married and made their lives in England, there was no chance we would ever live in Ireland again. I was devastated, but when I asked Dad about it he confirmed the agreement, so of course I grudgingly respected his wishes.

Life continued with school, home, and of course, church on Sundays. The priest, Father James, was young, good-looking and very charming. I have to admit that as a thirteen-year-old girl he was the only reason I enjoyed the service, and I remember thinking what a shame it was that he had given himself up to God—he would have made a lovely husband.

I once shared these thoughts with my mother, who was not amused in the slightest!

Before long, Father James broke the news he'd be moving to another parish. It wasn't just my teenage crush that left me feeling slightly numb at this news—I'd always felt a spiritual connection to him, and every week he made me feel special by coming over for a chat after he'd finished his sermon.

After he left, Harry chose to make me aware that there was a spiritualist church just over the road. Why hadn't I ever noticed it before?

"*You needed to meet Father James to know that there are good priests,*" Harry answered. "*But now, the choice is yours.*"

Curiosity overwhelmed me. I had a deep sense that the Catholic Church had served its purpose: my path led elsewhere.

The next Sunday I went to church as normal with Mum, plotting my escape. Halfway through the service, whilst my mother was deep in prayer with the rest of the congregation, I sneaked from my pew to join the spiritualist service.

Slipping quietly into a seat at the back of the room, I was surprised to see a woman taking the service. The atmosphere was calm and the room was dimly lit. I hadn't missed much; she started off with a prayer and then began giving messages from the other side.

I watched in amazement as the world I had been afraid to discuss for almost fourteen years was examined openly in public, with none of the shame or secrecy I had been made to feel by the Catholic Church. I don't think it had ever hit me until that moment just how suffocated I'd felt my entire life. I'd taken it all for granted: the unwritten rule to keep quiet about my gift, the pressure to be someone I was not, acceptance of the fact I was the "black sheep of the family." Nor had these things ever struck me as wrong; it was just the way things were. Now, suddenly, I saw another way, another path, another perspective on life—and it felt like coming home.

The messages from spirit were received with tears of joy: widows wept as their husbands, long departed from this plane, shared memories of holidays and special occasions through the medium. Skeptics would have had great difficulty explaining the events unfolding in the room as time and time again, the speaker passed on messages that defied logic: inherited amber jewelry locked in a chrome trinket box, knowledge of a baby boy aged eight months who had passed to spirit with heart problems, and comforting words of reassurance to a man who had lost his daughter in a tragic road accident.

My astonishment was compounded when the speaker looked directly at me and asked, "Who is Harry?"

I was bowled over and could only gasp, at which point I heard Harry's distinct chuckle in my head.

My heart was pounding and I didn't dare answer. The medium picked up on my fears about being considered crazy—I had become so used to that reaction it was impossible to shake—and she gently told me that one day, I would become very well known in the spiritualist movement.

"He's not the only one protecting you," she went on to say. "You are surrounded by spirit people." She smiled and gave me a knowing look. "But you're already aware of that, aren't you?"

There was a giggle from the rest of the congregation, who had turned in their seats to look at this red-faced, flabbergasted adolescent, and the speaker nodded. "I'll leave their love with you, dear," she said.

Turning away, the medium suddenly stopped and looked back at me. "But before I move on … it might be a good idea to tell your mother the truth. Dad's telling me she won't appreciate you leaving your Catholic Church to come and listen to me."

Another chortle from the congregation, and another knowing look from the medium. I don't remember the rest of the service, but I do know that what I'd experienced was to change my life. My face burning, my body tingling with excitement, a million thoughts raced through my head as I sat in stunned silence. What had taken me so long to discover this place?

Back at home, Mum's reaction was calmer than I'd expected. I told her about the spiritualist church, the messages relayed, and Dad's comment that I should be honest.

Mum looked at me for a while and then said, very matter-of-factly, "Well then. That's how it's going to be then, isn't it?"

And so it was.

On the third week of attending the spiritualist church I received another message, a warning that I had to be careful when walking home.

"Don't ever walk alone," the speaker told me. "I get the image of a bull in a field, which is symbolic of someone out to harm you. I don't mean to scare you, but please be very vigilant."

On that particular night, I was already feeling anxious about the journey home from church, so after the medium's warning, I asked Deirdre, a neighbour and member of the congregation, if she would accompany me.

As we neared my house, a young man of about twenty came into view. He was standing with his back to us in the entrance to an alleyway, and something about his presence gave me the creeps.

He was about five foot six and wearing scruffy, dark clothes: a hooded sweater and jeans.

The hairs on the back of my neck prickled up and I was overcome with a feeling of unease. Deirdre and I picked up our pace, moving closer together, and my father's voice came into my head: "*Keep calm now, Bridget.*"

As we were passing, the man turned quickly, grabbing me around the throat and dragging me into the alleyway. It all happened so fast that my memories are blurred, but I remember my father immediately stepped in to protect me. Deirdre was screaming for help and trying to pull me back to the street as I struggled and kicked to get free. My attacker didn't say a word during the scuffle. After what seemed like hours, we fought him off as best we could and the man eventually released me and ran away.

Shaken and bruised, Deirdre and I gave a description of the attacker to the police. His cold, hard face was etched into my mind and luckily, our photo-fit turned out to be very accurate. I felt sick to learn that the man had raped a young woman near my school some weeks earlier, and thankfully he was arrested and convicted for both attacks.

I kept this traumatic experience secret from my mother for months, from fear she would forbid me from attending the spiritualist church. The burden became too much, though, and one day I sat her down and nervously blurted out what had happened that night.

With tears running down her cheeks, Mum sat in silence until I had finished talking. Then she gave me a big hug and sobbed, "Thank God you have your dad looking after you, and Harry too." A wave of relief enveloped me and I clung to her for dear life as she stroked my hair.

I couldn't say I'm glad of the ordeal—I had insomnia for weeks and the man's sinister face haunted my dreams when I did eventually sleep—but they say every cloud has a silver lining, and in this case I felt much closer to Mum as a result of what I'd been through.

For the first time ever, she started to ask questions about the messages I received in church. Not only did Mum express an interest, but I knew that finally, my gift was accepted. She asked tentatively how often Dad spoke to me. I told her every day, and Harry as well.

After that, I felt a weight had been lifted from my shoulders, and now felt able to relay messages that were given to me about other family members who had passed, such as Grandma Kate and Granddad John, and I was able to tell Mum in detail how my life was so different to that of my brothers and sisters.

I once asked how she felt about my gift, and she surprised me again with a smile and some reassuring words.

"Bridget, your father predicted your birth at least six years before you were born," she said. "He taught me that I have to let you take your own path. It's not always easy for me, but that's how it is, and God works in mysterious ways."

"What else did Dad say?" I asked her.

Mum glanced at the floor and took a deep breath. "He told me, *All the children will be fine when I go*," she said quietly. "*But there will be a special thing with Bridget. You have to promise me that you will always listen to Bridget*."

I was so happy to hear this that for once, I was speechless. I threw my arms around Mum in unspoken gratitude, and went about the house with a huge smile for the rest of the week.

More good news came in 1969, when the farm was sold and we were able to move out of Kathleen's. Mum spent £600 on a two-bedroom back-to-back terrace with an outside toilet in nearby Rastrick. Kathleen's house was very modern in comparison, but we were thrilled to have our own place at last, whatever condition it was in. I felt a kind of stability for the first time in over a year.

I shared a bedroom with Rose and Mum, all three of us in one double bed, while Billy, reunited with Peter and Oliver, shared the other. It was very difficult to get any time to myself, so I tended to go to bed either before or after Mum and Rose, so I could continue my nightly chats with spirit.

Although we were all relieved to have some semblance of normality and be together once again, it was tough for Mum because she'd had a lot of help looking after us up until this point.

I remember we had no furniture, and all our clothes were still coming from the jumble sale. The milkman was very kind to us and used to give Mum her milk for free when money was really tight. It was very hard for her to get used to paying for things we used to get from the farm in Ireland: simple things like dairy, potatoes, and vegetables.

I used to babysit for a neighbour, which I loved because I had a whole house to myself, and I'd give Mum the pound I received to buy food. Rose was sixteen now and had a job as a shop clerk so she did the same. Peter and Oliver, despite only being eleven and ten, managed to find a milk round, so even they chipped into the family pot.

Billy stayed at home with Mum, and has done to this day. In Ireland there is a custom of "keeping one back" to look after ailing parents later in life, and in our family that sibling was Billy. He wasn't expected to work or marry, just to keep Mum company and care for her for the rest of her life. Although that sounds strange in modern times, it's quite the norm back in rural Ireland and the custom is rarely questioned.

I remember asking Mum if she would ever meet another man and try to be happy again. She looked at me with a blank face and answered, "Never." She had opportunities—she was very attractive and she could dance and sing very well. But Dad was the love of her life, and is to this day.

We continued to return to Ireland in every summer break, and it was a trip I looked forward to all year. Now I'd settled into school, the spirit children's classroom visits became less frequent, but I always saw them when I returned to Straide and it was glorious to see how they changed every year.

Lucy, my spirit friend from childhood, was turning into a young woman with me. Her freckles faded over time and she was becoming a beautiful flame-haired beauty, her Victorian clothing now flattering her fuller figure. I watched her change from girl to woman and felt it happening to me too. My hair was as auburn as hers—it didn't turn dark until later in life—and I had typical Irish looks, with my green eyes set into a face covered in freckles. I started wearing makeup, although Lucy's skin was flawless and she never needed it.

Lucy and I talked about normal teenage topics, about boys and secret crushes. Lucy was beautiful, but had never courted before she passed to spirit.

"*There were too many chores,*" she'd sigh, telling me how in life she would have to hurry home from school to polish the family crockery, or "delph" as she called it.

Being from the Victorian era it would have been impossible for Lucy to have a boyfriend anyway, although I always got the impression she would have been a heartbreaker in her earthly life and was probably loved by every boy in Straide!

At fifteen, I was allowed to attend village dances and Frank O'Reilly's and Jimmy Doherty's pubs, although I was expected to go with Mum, leave with Mum, and touch no alcohol.

Rose was courting her husband at the time so she never came to Ireland with us, which meant Mum kept a very close eye on me. As a typical teenager, this annoyed me and made me feel suffocated, but the village dances were such fun I soon forgot.

The fiddlers would play Irish jigs and everybody would be up and dancing, twirling and laughing. Dad had taught me how to waltz, and we also danced the Stackabarley, which was rather like line dancing. I used to always get up and sing too.

That summer, 1971, I went back to the shop in Ballyvary where my life had changed in one phone call. Ann Maloney hugged me and burst into tears, and I sobbed too; it brought it all back. She had lost her husband that year, so it was a very emotional reunion. For old times' sake, I fetched her some water from the pump.

CHAPTER
8

Back in England, I had started to become interested in boys. The only problem was, once I met someone I liked, I immediately felt my relationship with the spirit world was being invaded.

For years I had sat and communicated with the other side at every opportunity: in the hay fields and the peat bogs, at school and under the gooseberry bush, in my bedroom and in the classroom—whenever I was alone. And although I was interested in growing up and developing relationships, I hadn't anticipated losing that part of my life simply because I was courting.

Both Peter and Oliver were involved with the St. John's Ambulance, and I became acquainted with an eighteen-year-old cadet named David. I think he was a lot keener on me than I was on him, but he was a lovely boy and funnily enough, my mother loved him to bits.

David talked a lot about how he intended on marrying me, but my gut feeling told me he would have an early passing. The more he talked of us being husband and wife, the more I felt I couldn't lead him on, and I was beginning to get irritated with him being at the house so often because—in truth—I preferred speaking to spirit.

One night, as David launched into another monologue about our future wedding, I couldn't keep quiet any longer.

"David, we're not going to get married," I blurted out.

Knowing about my gift, David looked at me for a while, then asked quietly, "What do you see then?"

I took a deep breath. "I see your time on Earth is only short," I told him softly. "I can't give you what you want. I'm sorry, I need to let you go."

I broke his heart that day. But true to his gentle nature, he never held a grudge. Shortly after we parted ways, he began seeing a lady twenty years his senior, and they married and went on to have a daughter.

That baby girl never knew her father. David passed to spirit in January 1975, just twenty-one years old.

My second relationship was very different; I was so in love I would have given up everything for one more minute with Paddy Donohue.

We met when I was sweet sixteen, while I was in Ireland with my family on another long summer holiday.

It was 1972 and I was enjoying the music in O'Reilly's with family. In England I was into Tamla Motown, but back home all we ever listened to was traditional Irish band music.

The pub was busy, with men playing tin whistles, fiddles, harmonicas, and accordions, and everybody up dancing or clapping and drumming on the table in time. At the end of one jig, I pushed through the crowd of laughing, rowdy locals and headed for the bathroom.

Paddy was perched at the bar, wearing a white shirt with a navy-blue suit and matching tie. He was tall, slim, and good-looking: shoulder-length blonde hair and straight, white teeth. Amongst the usual country folk gathered around the bar in their work clothes, he stood out a mile and my stomach flipped over at the very sight of him. It was unusual to see somebody I didn't know in the village, and I was desperate to find out who this gorgeous man was.

As if he'd picked up on my thoughts, his blue eyes caught mine and my butterflies intensified. I had never had a feeling like it.

I had turned into a typical Irish colleen, my long wavy locks framing a pretty face with piercing green eyes. I was tall and slim, wearing black trousers and a bell-sleeved shirt teamed with a trendy tank top.

I never did go to the bathroom. As I brushed past the mystery man he made a compliment about my appearance and I stopped to give him a shy smile. My heart was pounding, my cheeks burning. The way he looked me up and down spoke volumes—and we didn't need to exchange words to know the attraction was mutual.

Paddy introduced himself and asked my name, and instantly I felt like I had known him forever. He was twenty-one and worked in civil engineering. Paddy had been living in Birmingham but had ended a relationship to return to Ireland and care for his mother who had fallen ill. I told him I lived in England too, and felt close enough to talk about the death of my dad. He was very sympathetic; his own father had passed when he was just nine years old.

From that point we seemed to have so much in common, I lost track of time and never returned to sit with my mother and the rest of the family—though I kept glancing over to see her watching me and she was not looking impressed!

Mum's weren't the only eyes boring into the side of my head. I could sense the burning stares of every girl in the pub. They all wanted to be standing where I was. Paddy noticed this too and he took my hand and gave it a squeeze, with a grin that sent my stomach flipping over again.

"Don't worry about that," he reassured me with his twinkling eyes and a sideways nod of the head to a group of whispering girls. "I want you to talk to me. Stay."

So I did. Despite my mother's protests, I let Paddy walk me home to Frank O'Reilly's bungalow, where we were staying.

The sky was as clear as ever, the moonlight and hundreds of stars shining down on us as we wandered hand in hand through the maze of *boreens*. I felt like a princess in a magical romantic fairytale and I walked slowly, not wanting the night to ever end.

Paddy stopped and removed his jacket, tenderly draping it over my shoulders to keep me warm. He looked deep into my eyes and then leaned in to kiss me. I thought my heart would stop beating, it skipped around my chest so much! I'd kissed boys before, but never had I felt exhilaration like this. I remember thinking that this was it, this was the real thing; love at first sight does exist.

I went to bed that night with a huge smile on my face, playing the night over and over in my mind, daydreaming of what our next meeting would bring and thinking desperately of ways Paddy and I could be together in the future.

For the next two weeks we were inseparable and I was the envy of every girl in the village. I saw him nearly every night; we met in the pub and would sit holding hands and kissing. My mother was always present, sitting on a corner table with a sour face, casting disapproving looks in our direction. But I didn't care. Those moments would stay with me forever.

Every day I'd get a scolding from Mum, who told me in no uncertain terms that our relationship had no future. I was due to start my nursing training in England that September, and Mum never tired of reminding me of this childhood ambition and how important it was not to jeopardize it.

I couldn't understand why she was so protective of me, but looking back I suppose I was the most outgoing and strong willed of us all. She was scared that love would pull me away from the family—after all, she had fallen for Dad at the same age.

I tried to take Mum's feelings into account, but I was secretly determined to enjoy my time with Paddy, whatever the consequences. The holiday flew by. Every night I dreaded leaving him to return to the bungalow, another precious day lost to the march of time and my imminent return to England.

On our last night together, Paddy told me he felt like he'd met me in a past life and we had a special bond.

"Would you ever move back to Ireland?" He asked me softly as we curled up together on the floor of a hay shed, hiding from the world.

Nothing happened in that barn; cuddling and talking were enough for us both. I took his hand and thinking of what my mother had said, I told him that I would return, as soon as I was old enough to make my own decisions.

"If you come back I'd like to see you. Properly." Paddy whispered as he pushed a wisp of hair from my eyes. The thought of leaving him was unbearable.

We exchanged addresses and both promised to write. Neither of us wanted to let go, so he didn't walk me home until 4 a.m. Letting go of his hand and kissing him for the last time was too much.

He told me to think of him in two weeks' time on his birthday, and to expect a letter soon, then he disappeared into the darkness. I watched him go, trying to remember every detail of him, before eventually returning to the bungalow with a heavy heart to find my mother and a friend looking for me.

I was in big trouble; we had to catch a train from Castlebar in just a few hours that morning. I can't remember my punishment, but I know it was trivial in comparison to my pain over leaving Paddy. I cried non-stop all the way back to England: on the four-hour train journey to Dublin, the ferry ride to Liverpool, and all the way back up to Yorkshire.

My mother was less than sympathetic and told me to pull myself together. I remember a stranger on the train seemed concerned and asked me what was wrong, but I couldn't answer him. I just closed my eyes and wrapped myself in the memory of Paddy's embrace.

The first thing I did when I got home was to empty my suitcase out and inhale the smell of my clothes. The hay from the barn on our last night together and Paddy's scent brought it all back. Tears welled in my eyes and I spent hours sobbing into the top I'd been wearing when we parted.

That day, I wrote a letter telling Paddy how much he had affected me in that fleeting time we'd spent together, and that it was the best holiday I had ever had. Every day I waited excitedly for the postman to deliver his reply, but none came. After a few weeks, my gut instincts were telling me that he'd written back but I had never been given the letter. I wrote again, but heard nothing. I felt miserable and heartbroken and decided I had to get on with my life—perhaps he hadn't felt the same after all. But for a long time, Paddy was on my mind at some part of the day, and my suspicions about family interference never left me.

That was the last of those long, hot summers when Mum took me to Ireland with her, and I never saw Paddy again until October 2008, thirty-six years after our holiday romance. He recognized me immediately and came over for a talk in O'Reilly's in Ballyvary, where it all began. It was wonderful to see him again.

Paddy said he had written to me religiously in the months after we parted: my mother had never given me the letters.

In April 1974, eighteen months after my romance with Paddy, I met my future husband, Kenn. I was seventeen and partway through my nursing training. I have to say, I was still heartbroken over my Irish love—the last thing on my mind was another relationship. But it seemed silly to pine over him any longer, so I had decided to throw myself into my career and try to enjoy myself at weekends in an attempt to put the past behind me.

One night I went out with some college friends to the Bull's Head pub in Halifax. There was a group of young men at the bar, and as we ordered our drinks I could feel one of them looking at me intensely. Turning, I saw a handsome chap with kind, sparkling blue eyes. He didn't look away when I caught him—he smiled, and I noticed he had lovely teeth. He reminded me a lot of Paddy.

The pub was a regular place for hospital staff to meet and every time I went, the young man was there, slying glances at me from across the bar. I discovered his name was Kenn and he was a chef at the Royal Infirmary, where I was due to start my nursing placement that September.

Kenn's friends knew mine and we began to see each other regularly on nights out; it was difficult to avoid him now we were in the same circle. I was attracted to Kenn and knew he felt the same—he'd already asked if he could take me out—but my feelings were still raw from my Irish love, and I was determined not to get involved with anyone.

A couple of weeks after I'd first seen him, I was dancing on stage with my friends to Tamla Motown and Status Quo. I was wearing hotpants and long silver boots, and my long auburn hair was loose and wavy.

I could see Kenn with another girl at the bar. She hung on his every word and was quite obviously interested in him. I was surprised to feel a pang of jealousy. Kenn looked up and caught my eye before making his excuses to his admirer and weaving his way through the crowd to talk to me.

"Hello, you," Kenn grinned as he shouted over the music. My heart skipped.

"I need some help," he told me. "That girl over there won't leave me alone. Do you think you're brave enough to rescue me?"

Relieved they weren't attached, I laughed and agreed to come up with a plan. Kenn thanked me and returned to the girl at the bar, who looked very pleased to have him back. What I didn't know was that he had already made a date with her, and had only changed his mind after he'd seen me walk into the pub.

So, I borrowed a ring from my friend, put it on my engagement finger and walked over to the pair of them.

"What do you think you're playing at?" I asked Kenn, trying to sound as angry as possible.

His date looked confused.

"This is my fiancé," I told her, pointing at Kenn. He was doing a great job of looking like a rabbit caught in the headlights!

The woman looked furious and, without giving Kenn a chance to explain, she muttered a few expletives before hitting him and storming off to the ladies room.

I felt bad for her and was quite annoyed once it had become clear Kenn had led her on, but it seemed I was stuck with him for the rest of the evening whether I liked it or not.

That night, Kenn walked me to my bus stop and leaned in for a kiss. I wasn't ready for a relationship and held back, but at the same time I felt it was fate that we met: to me, it was more than coincidence we would be working at the infirmary together that autumn.

The weekend came, and Kenn's eyes lit up as I entered the pub. He asked if he could buy me a drink and I agreed to a coca cola.

When he opened his wallet I noticed a photograph of a blonde girl and my mind flashed back to the week before. Was Kenn really available?

"*All will become clear,*" Harry told me.

"Who's that?" I demanded.

Kenn looked sheepish and took a deep breath.

"I'm engaged, Bridget," he admitted. "We're due to marry this June, but after meeting you I've realised I can't go ahead with it. I'm going to call it off."

I was shocked and didn't know how to react. On the one hand I was flattered at his feelings for me, but I felt to blame for his broken engagement, and angry that he hadn't been honest with me from the start.

"No, Kenn, please don't do that on my account," I begged him. "We don't know each other that well, and apart from anything else, I'm Catholic and you're Protestant—it will never work. You should have told me this before, you've put me in a really difficult situation."

Kenn looked upset, but brushed aside my concerns.

"I know all that," he mumbled. "But as soon as I saw you I wanted you. I can't marry someone else; it wouldn't be fair. I want to get to know you better, Bridget."

I was confused and spent most of the night with friends, ignoring Kenn's glances at me from across the room.

After a few more times of meeting, always at the Bull's Head, Kenn told me that he had now broken off his engagement. He had worked as a chef in the Army, which is where he had met his fiancée. She was called Janet, and was supposed to be coming over from Hong Kong to live with Kenn.

"I told her over the phone," he said one night. "I just can't go through with it. She's flying over to try to sort things out."

"In that case, you should try to repair it," I told him.

He looked at me sadly.

"I don't want any part of this, Kenn," I said sternly. "She obviously loves you very much. Please talk to her. Good luck."

I turned and left, pausing at the door to look back at Kenn. He looked upset and full of regrets.

With a heavy heart, I left the pub and tried to enjoy the rest of my night. If we are meant to be, then we will be, I told myself. I was still annoyed at his dishonesty, but a feeling of excitement overruled any negative emotions: I knew deep down that this wasn't the end, only the beginning.

CHAPTER 9

My intuition was right. At the beginning of June, just before my eighteenth birthday and the month Kenn would have been marrying another woman, a message came through our mutual friend Kay that he wanted to take me out. I'd missed seeing his smiling face, our talks, the way he made me feel so special. Our first proper date ... I decided to bite the bullet and agreed to meet up with him.

I walked into the pub feeling nervous, but Kenn was nowhere to be seen. Anxious I'd been stood up, I seated myself at the bar and ordered a drink, feeling very self-conscious without my friends.

To my relief, Kay rushed into the pub soon after. But the look on her face didn't convince me the news was good.

"Kenn's had an accident," she told me breathlessly. "He told me to come and meet you—he's in hospital."

"What happened?" I asked, my voice cracking as I feared the worst.

"Don't panic, they think he'll be okay," Kay reassured me. "But it was bad. He was coming home from work today and was knocked off his motorbike by a bus."

I slammed down my drink and scooped up my handbag.

"I'm going straight there," I told her, and rushed out, hoping a taxi was free and feeling sick to the stomach.

Kenn looked terrible. His face was bruised and battered, his collarbone and wrist were broken and he was semi-conscious with a drip in his arm. But true to form, he still managed to give me a smile.

"You came," he said weakly.

"Yes. Don't try to talk."

I took his hand and felt a surge of emotion. Was this meant to be? Surely not. Perhaps it had been a mistake to come, and Kenn was never the one. *Why would this happen on our first date?* I asked myself. But I knew I was brushing my feelings under the carpet. Watching him drift in and out of sleep in the hospital bed, it hit me that Kenn meant far more to me than I had imagined.

I left the ward feeling sad. Neither of us had telephones at the time, so once again I was unsure whether I would see Kenn again or whether our date would ever come to pass.

Apart from Harry's whispered message that all would become clear, spirit gave me no more clues. It was almost as if our fate was undecided at that time, or for some reason I was not meant to know. My gut feelings were so jumbled and confused I couldn't think clearly, but not long after, another set of unfortunate circumstances would join our paths for a second time.

On my eighteenth birthday, I saw Kenn in the pub. He looked much better and I was thrilled he was up and about, well enough to socialise with friends.

Kenn grinned and waved and I smiled back and made my way over to him

"Happy birthday," Kenn said softly. He gave me a hug before handing me a card and gift—a bottle of perfume. I was so flattered that he'd remembered and gone to the trouble, especially after all he'd been through. So there in the middle of the pub, we finally had our first kiss. I desperately wanted to stay with him, but I'd made plans to go to a nightclub with my nursing friends.

I was an adult, and free at last from my mother's curfews. It was the first time I had ever gone out and been given permission to stay at a friend's rather than catching an early bus home to share a room with Mum. My relationship with her had changed little; she was a traditionalist and until the night of my eighteenth I was under her watch and unable to make my own decisions. Now, I felt free and ecstatic, buoyed by Kenn's recovery and our kiss.

But my celebrations were not meant to be. An hour or so later, I collapsed with a pain down my left side and was in agony. I was taken to casualty, and was told the police had visited my mother to let her know I was in hospital. The thought of her reaction terrified me and certainly sobered me up quickly!

After being quizzed about whether I had taken drugs and then asked if I was losing a baby, both of which I found very offensive and upsetting, in the early hours of the morning a doctor finally diagnosed me with ovarian cysts.

"I'm very sorry to have to tell you this, but you have polycystic ovaries and it's likely you will never be able to conceive naturally," the doctor told me gently.

This was confirmed after a scan: I was told there was no hope whatsoever.

I was in deep shock. My world fell apart and I sobbed into my pillow as I considered this bombshell. My intuition told me it wasn't true, but in my grief—and with the pain-killers clouding my judgement—I thought maybe I was in denial.

Kenn came to visit me as soon as he heard the news, by which point I'd made my mind up.

"I can't see you again," I wept. "You should never have broken off your engagement for me, nothing has happened with us yet and we should end it before it gets serious."

Kenn looked shocked and tears welled in his eyes. "No," he shook his head firmly. "I'm not letting go, children or not. I've loved you from the first time I saw you and I won't give up."

We talked for some time. I was taken aback with his level of feeling for me, and nothing I said seemed to change his mind.

"I need to think," I told him, and we parted on that note.

After he'd left, I lay in bed considering the events of the night. Harry's and Dad's laughter came into my head.

"*This could only happen to you,*" Harry chuckled.

I couldn't believe they were making light of it, but Dad cut in: "*Ignore the doctors, Bridget. You will have two boys and a girl. Pull yourself together, it's going to be fine.*"

I wiped away my tears and felt a wave of comfort wash over my body. I was too tired and overwhelmed to ask any questions, but I didn't need to: Dad was never wrong. I slept like a baby, clinging to that message as I dreamed.

I didn't see Kenn for a couple of weeks, but when I did, I agreed to take things slowly. I trusted my father's message more than the medical profession, despite training to be a nurse myself!

In November, Kenn arranged to take me and some friends to the seaside resort of Blackpool for the day. Two days before we went, I caught chickenpox while working as an auxiliary on the children's ward. I was very ill, and just as I was recovering from the first illness, I contracted mumps. My weight plummeted to just below nine stones, and at a willowy five feet ten inches, I looked a sorry state.

After this setback I gave up on Kenn. There were too many obstacles in our way, and I felt that fate was trying to tell us we weren't meant for one another.

Despite my doubts, Kenn never stopped pursuing me. A week later, while I was in bed at home, there was a knock on my door and my mother answered it to find Kenn on the doorstep. He'd got my address from a colleague and seemed so concerned for my health I didn't have the heart—or the strength—to discuss my decision to end the relationship. On top of that, he'd bought me another gift—this time a record: "I'd Love You to Want Me, The Way That I Want You."

He didn't stay long, but promised to return when I was feeling well enough for visitors.

Kenn's appearance caused a barrage of questions from my mother, all of which I was too weak to answer. I'd never spoken of him because his Protestant background was still a concern, but Mum wanted to know who he was, where we'd met, what kind of a man he was.

I told her it was nothing serious, convinced that he'd soon change his mind about pursuing me, but he never did. He returned a few days later, and his persistence never ceased to amaze me.

Once I'd recovered, I met up with friends in Halifax. It was the 20th December 1974 and I saw Kenn in the usual bar. I was over the moon when he asked the DJ to play a song for me: "You're my First, My Last, My Everything," by Barry White.

After my song was finished, Kenn got down on one knee and took my hand.

"Bridget O'Malley, will you marry me?"

I gasped as our friends whooped and cheered around us. What could I say? I still had my doubts, but it hit me that I was falling in love. It was futile to stop it.

"Yes," I whispered, and Kenn jumped up and gave me a bear hug as the pub erupted around us. I felt like life couldn't get any better; my fiancé was fantastic, a best friend who I could talk to about anything. My family grew to love Kenn in spite of the religious differences, and I got on very well with his parents, Cyril and Penny, too.

His paternal grandmother was Betty, a wonderful, charismatic lady who was to play a crucial role in my life. But we didn't hit it off immediately. I always got the distinct impression Betty disliked me and the feeling was mutual: Betty smoked a lot and I hated the fact she allowed the ash from her cigarette to fall on the carpet and then rub it in with her shoe. She also seemed to suffer with a lot of wind! But Kenn absolutely adored her, so I tried to be as polite and friendly as possible.

As time went by, these things became irrelevant to me; they were all part of Betty's eccentric nature. We found we had a lot in common with our interest in spiritualism, and we would discuss this topic for hours every Sunday when Kenn and I had lunch at his parent's house. Betty often told me she felt our paths had crossed in a previous life.

On Christmas Day 1975, Betty, Kenn, Penny, Cyril, and I were seated at the table, ready to tuck into our lunch. Betty had been out and had a good drink before placing herself at the head of the table.

"I have something for your wedding," she announced, piling potatoes on to her plate.

Kenn and I exchanged glances.

"Our wedding's nearly a year away, Gran," Kenn chuckled. "I think you've had too much to drink!" We all laughed, but Betty shook her head and her face remained serious.

She pulled back her chair and went into the kitchen, returning with a black leather box.

"There you go," she said, placing it between Kenn and I.

"Go on, open it then!"

We did as we were told, and inside was a beautiful silver cutlery set: fish knives, forks, and gleaming spoons.

"Betty this is lovely," I told her. "But you don't have to."

"Yes I do," Betty interrupted, back in her seat and cutting into her food.

"I won't be there for the wedding. I'll be in heaven, looking down on you."

There was a stunned silence and my eyes welled with tears. Kenn and his parents, knowing her as they did, never argued. And of course I never doubted her word; it brought back painful memories of my father correctly predicting his own passing all those years before. I managed to whisper a small "thank you," and Kenn quietly told her he loved her very much.

"Don't mention it," Betty told him with a smile. She turned to me and waved her fork in my direction.

"I'll be working with you Bridget," she told me. "So don't get upset; we'll be talking as much as we always have."

Betty continued eating as I waited for her to explain.

"Of course, I can't read or write," she said, chewing as she spoke. "But I can still help you in your line of work, can't I?"

She looked at me with twinkling eyes and swiftly moved on to the next topic, as though this was nothing out of the ordinary.

Betty passed to spirit on the 5th September 1976 with a pulmonary embolism. Her death was so sudden it would have been impossible for even medical professionals to predict.

Since that day, she has kept her promise to work with me: Betty turned out to be the best spirit guide a clairvoyant medium could wish to have, as I would find out in the years that followed.

CHAPTER

10

Kenn and I married on 23rd October 1976, a month after Betty's prediction of her own death came to pass.

My dress was classic white with a long, flowing veil. It was a big Catholic wedding, which pleased my mother of course, and I had decided my brother John would give me away—he reminds me so much of Dad he was the obvious choice.

When Kenn and I walked into the reception greeted by well-wishers, I caught sight of a table overflowing with wedding gifts. At the top of the pile was Betty's present, which had been wrapped up for us to open again.

It was a beautiful day, but clouded by our loss. I would have given anything to see her standing there, cigarette ash toppling on to the carpet. It's funny how those of us who have faith in the spirit world are susceptible to grief and loss in exactly the same way as anyone else: I even missed the things that annoyed me most about Betty.

Kenn and I danced to *Ave Maria*, my head resting on his shoulder as our guests took photographs of the happy couple.

"*This is my favourite song,*" Betty's voice told me as clear as day. It was a wonderful relief to know she was there celebrating with us, and had even helped with the music choices!

The reception went on well into the night and it really was the happiest day of my life.

I thought of my father and how proud he would have been, and as Kenn and I got ready to leave I heard Dad's voice in my head: "*You've got a good one there, Bridget.*" I grinned, my heart leaping. His blessing was the icing on the cake, a wonderful end to a beautiful day.

I qualified as a nurse in November 1976 and worked in orthopaedics at the Halifax Infirmary. Kenn was promoted to assistant head chef at the hospital, and in October 1978 I found out I was pregnant. I was overjoyed that the doctors had been proven wrong about my infertility, and my faith in spirit was reinforced that day; life couldn't get any better.

But one day in January 1979 while I was pregnant, Kenn woke up in a shaken state, telling me he'd had a dream that our good friend John had died in a house fire. We got up and dressed, intending on going round to John's to check up on him, when the hospital called. It was Cathy, a colleague of mine.

She told us that John's body had been brought into casualty that morning. He had died a week earlier of carbon monoxide poisoning, aged twenty-eight. He had only just been found, asleep on the sofa.

I was distraught, but my emotions were nothing compared to Kenn's. The tragedy hit my husband hard; he was subdued and distant for weeks. Not only was he shocked and devastated about the passing of a close friend, he was confused as to why John's passing had been shown to him in his dream.

Kenn was also upset that I hadn't seen it coming. Why, he asked, would a close friend's early and tragic death escape my attention? Kenn's accusatory tone left me feeling incredibly guilty, but I can only assume spirit didn't pass the information on because I had specifically requested that they give me only good news while I was pregnant.

I explained to Kenn that he should treat his dream as proof of the spirit world's existence. "I hope this means you'll have some faith in the messages we're given," I told him gently. I rubbed my bump. "They've told me it's a boy," I said. "Then I'll have a girl, then another boy."

Kenn rolled his eyes, clearly not in the mood to discuss it. I decided to give him time to grieve—he'd see soon enough.

Not only had my children's births been foretold by Dad in my hospital bed when I was eighteen, but they had also been confirmed by some gypsies I'd met during my nursing training. It was May 1975 and I was shopping for wedding dresses in nearby Bradford with my friends Steph and Fran (who was due to tie the knot that summer), when a middle-aged lady and two young girls approached us.

All of them had long flowing ebony hair tied back loosely, and were wearing ankle-length traditional skirts and psychedelic tops. The older lady had a traveller's headscarf wrapped around her black locks, and the younger girls had sallow, freckled skin.

I felt like I knew them, but I wasn't sure whether the reaction was negative or not. A cold shiver swept down my spine.

"Can we talk to yas?"

Their accent was unusual, but unmistakably Irish.

My friends and I were in a rush, but exchanged glances and reluctantly agreed to stop for a moment. The gypsies didn't seem interested in Steph or Fran; it was as if they were invisible. All three women stared intently at me with their piercing green eyes.

The older told me I would have a boy, then a girl, then another boy. My eldest son would be extremely talented with music, but his main occupation would involve his other passion: drawing.

My daughter would be a twin, but only she would survive full term.

"The little boy from that pregnancy will return to spirit," the lady predicted.

I was told my daughter wouldn't have the same academic mind as the other two, but she would be a loyal person and a good listener. She would go on to use her natural nursing abilities to work with children.

My youngest son, who would be born after a long gap in pregnancies, would not only be a good musician, but would excel at every sport he tried. Water sports in particular would be his passion—diving, swimming, and canoeing. This third child would replace my daughter's twin.

The gypsies told me they could see that I wore a uniform, and that I was very intuitive.

"One day people will see you in that light," the older woman said.

I smiled to myself as I thanked them and walked away, knowing that what the older traveller had told me was true. I had never doubted what spirit had told me, but it was nice to hear it from another source. Discussing the messages, my friends and I went about our business, and for the rest of the day, I was excited to return home and tell Kenn I had more proof I was able to be a mum one day.

Now, carrying the son the gypsies had spoken of, John's passing made it incredibly difficult to look forward to the birth—the only way I could cope was to tell myself I would hear from him again.

Luckily I have, several times, since his life was cut so short. John visited me before his funeral, just to let us know that he had arrived safely and nobody was to blame. It's always such a comfort to hear this from those we've lost, and I only wish we all had the gift and could see our loved ones as they are in spirit: free from suffering and, clichéd as it sounds, in a much better place.

The remainder of my pregnancy passed without tragedy and on the 10th July, I went into hospital and was induced that evening.

It was a very emotional time—knowing I was going to have my baby, proving the doctors wrong. Kenn was still skeptical we'd have a boy—after all there was no proof other than from spirit that he would be male—but there wasn't a doubt in my mind.

I coped well with the pain and Kenn was as supportive as ever. My labour continued through the night, and Mathew was born on Wednesday 11th July 1979 at 5:50 a.m., weighing seven pounds.

He was beautiful, with lots of very dark hair and a sallow complexion, and was an adorable and easy-going baby.

I went back to work on nights two days a week when Mathew was four months old, with Kenn staying at home to look after him.

Working as a nurse definitely developed my gift. I knew intuitively who was next to pass: I often saw spirit people coming to the ward to take their loved ones to the next world. On odd occasions, nobody from spirit seemed to be there, in which case I made sure I was around to hold the patient's hand. It was certainly a useful gift to know who needed comforting before they left this plane.

Many of the patients talked about "leaving" immediately before they passed over, and they would often reach out to family members whose forms were there to guide them. Then, at the moment of death, I often saw the separation of body and spirit—the vital life energy that makes us conscious—flowing upward and dissipating into the air, just as the machines flatlined.

The other nurses used to ask me who the patients were talking to or reaching out to. More often than not they trusted my instincts, so together we made a great team and were always well prepared on the ward.

Sometimes, we had up to three deaths in any one shift. It was a very busy ward with thirty-nine beds, and just as the spirit children had helped me on the farm all those years before, I felt I was being helped as a nurse by the other side.

Back when I was first training to be a nurse in 1974, we spent a lot of time at college learning and writing. After the first month, we went on to the ward. My first experience of hospital work was on a surgical ward, and I wore a green striped uniform, a crisp white apron, and a white cap embossed with a green stripe.

It was December, and I was working over the festive period. On Christmas Day morning I went onto the ward but felt uneasy; there was an eerie feeling about the place and I was apprehensive.

I was told that a cancer patient of ours, Mark, had deteriorated over the last couple of days and had become critically ill. I knew immediately that he would pass to spirit and I was upset—he was only thirty-six and would leave behind a wife and little girl. Just as we were about to serve Christmas lunch, Mark passed over.

That was the first time I had ever seen it happen: his maternal grandmother and grandfather came to meet him from spirit and help him pass over safely. My body tingled with goosebumps as I watched. His spirit family, invisible to Mark and everyone else, stood quietly and solemnly by the bed as the machines bleeped and the medical staff, bustling and frantic, unaware of these unfolding events, scrambled to save Mark's life. I remember trying to get on with my work as Mark's soul, bright white and ethereal, left his body and his grandparents—their features as clear as day but with fuzzy, blurred outlines—lovingly took his hands and instantly disappeared from vision. I gasped, my heart pounding, my legs turning to jelly.

"We've lost him," I heard a colleague say, as if from a place far away.

I was devastated. It didn't seem to matter that I had seen him leave, that I knew he was in a better place with no pain—my experience had shaken me badly, and thinking of his poor family, alone at Christmas, brought back my own painful memories of Dad's passing.

That night I became sick and ended up staying in hospital overnight with tonsillitis. Even though I felt I had coped well, it became clear to me that it would take a while to harden myself to hospital life.

One thing I did feel confident about was the healing I gave to patients, unbeknownst to the ward sister. I never told the patients what I was doing as I took their hands in mine, but invariably they would feel much better—a few who were interested in spiritualism seemed to understand what I was doing, although we never spoke of it. Just as it had been with Dad as a child, my hands became hot as I felt the energy leaving my own body and transferring to theirs. The patients' skin seemed to glow with renewed energy and vitality, as though whatever makes us live had begun to flow again. It is a very tiring and draining process, though, and I was left exhausted and faint every time I gave healing.

One night, an elderly lady called Rebecca was admitted with a broken hip. We all heard her speaking to herself in the night: the other nurses thought she was confused but I knew she was talking to spirit. I became close to her. One night she took my hand and told me, "David wants you to know he's okay."

David, the first boy I had courted, was one of the few people I had attempted to connect with and failed. I had felt him around me and sensed he wanted to say something, but for some reason a message was never forthcoming. It was lovely hearing from him and having Rebecca on the ward, and as a result we spoke a lot and developed a strong bond.

All the nurses were very intrigued by my work and I found myself giving readings when we were less busy. I gave readings to all the nurses, but one message in particular stands out in my memory.

I was given some German tarot cards around this time, and used them one day to give a reading to my colleague Jean. I saw the usual things: career news, house moves, holidays abroad, and that her son Bobby would marry and have a baby. Then I suddenly had an image of him in a horrific motorbike accident.

"Jean, I don't know how to say this," I began. "But although there's a lot of happiness on the cards, there's also a warning. Please tell Bobby to be very careful on his motor-bike, won't you?"

Jean's eyes widened. "Oh God, what can you see?" She asked, clutching my arm. I shook my head: I couldn't possibly describe the scene that had just flashed through my mind.

"Just do your best to persuade him not to ride it," I said. "Or at least to be extra vigilant, that's all," I reassured her, hoping desperately that this would be enough to prevent my premonition.

But sadly it wasn't. Not long after the card reading, Bobby was on the motorway and was hit by a foreign truck driver, who was on the wrong side of the road. Paralysed from the neck down, Bobby was lucky to survive at all, but he did pull through and went on to marry and have a child as I predicted.

Life continued as normal. Kenn and I were happy, we had a lovely home and a beautiful baby boy and I loved my work as a nurse. But late one night in December 1979, when Mathew was five months old, I suddenly had an overwhelming feeling that I needed to go home from work. I felt sick, agitated and uncomfortable.

"What am I feeling?" I asked Betty.

"*Kay is with Kenn at your house,*" came the reply.

I gasped, my stomach turning over as I saw a clear mental image of my husband with Kay: a very close friend of mine, she had been the bridesmaid at our wedding and was the ex-wife of our departed friend John.

I shouldn't have been home until after nine o'clock the next morning, but I managed to make my excuses and leave early, getting a lift home from a colleague. I had a heavy feeling of dread and my heart was hammering in my chest.

When I went to put the key in the door I realised I'd been locked out from the inside, but peering through the window I saw Kenn asleep on the couch. I knocked on the door and he woke up, looking surprised and flustered to see me. As he let me in, I noticed that Kay's coat and handbag were over the chair downstairs, and pushing past Kenn, I ran upstairs and found her in my bed. She was wearing one of my nightgowns, but her underwear was hanging on the end of the marital bed.

I'm sorry to say that I completely lost it.

"Get out of my house," I screamed at Kay. She was half asleep and didn't seem to know what was going on, but I had my hands around her throat so she was finding it difficult to talk or fight me off. Kenn had chased me upstairs and he was shouting at me to let go, trying to drag me off Kay.

Spirit was trying to tell me to calm down, but I wasn't listening.

"*Ask them for an explanation,*" I heard Betty say, as I threw Kay out of the bedroom.

But Kay left, and Kenn was too angry to discuss anything with me. He has always vehemently denied cheating on me, but I have never to this day had an explanation from Kay, and we never spoke again.

I still loved Kenn, and I made the difficult decision to carry on with life as normal. As a Catholic, my vows were important to me and I believed that marriage was forever, for better or worse. It wasn't easy; after that night the trust had gone and I felt there was a void between us that would be difficult to repair. But Kenn was my husband, and I was sticking with him.

Time went by and I'd had difficulty conceiving; we had been trying for two years and I was beginning to lose hope. In summer 1983, however, I missed a period and was thrilled. But when the doctor did a pregnancy test it came back negative.

"*Don't listen to them, you are having a baby,*" came Dad's voice as I walked out of the surgery feeling deflated.

A month or so later, around September, I decided to conduct a séance. I do this by sitting at a table, closing my eyes, and posing a specific question in my mind which I then focus on through meditation. I then ask my guides to help me find the answers and guide me in the right direction.

That particular day, I was focusing on Dad's message and my negative pregnancy test, and before I'd had a chance to call on my guides for help, Betty's voice came through, clear as day.

"*Congratulations on the impending birth of your daughter, Elizabeth,*" She told me.

I gasped. "So it's true what Dad said?" I asked her excitedly.

"*Oh, yes,*" Betty confirmed. "*But it will be a sad time too, Bridget. She is one of two babies you're carrying, but you will only give birth to your daughter.*"

I thought of the gypsy's message all those years earlier. Despite the negative test, I trusted Betty's words one hundred percent.

That weekend I went for another pregnancy test and this time it was positive. Kenn and I were thrilled, as were his parents.

But Betty and the gypsies were also correct about the tragedy that was to unfold during the course of the pregnancy. At sixteen weeks, I went into hospital with suspected appendicitis after having severe abdominal pain.

The surgeon told me it wasn't my appendix; it was a gynaecological problem. I had miscarried a little boy, whom I later named Charles Daniel, after my father.

"What about my other baby?" I asked the doctor.

They looked confused.

"There's only one baby, Mrs. Benson." I was told gently. "And I'm afraid you've lost it."

"No," I told them firmly. "I was carrying twins."

Kenn tried to persuade me to let it go, but I knew the gypsies and my spirit guides were right. We left the hospital the next day with the medical staff thinking I was crazy, but I was adamant I was still pregnant with my little girl.

A few weeks went by, and I wasn't getting any bigger. My friends and family began to worry as I refused to let the matter lie.

"You're deluding yourself," Kenn told me. "I'm grieving for the baby too, Bridget, but let's just move on and try again."

I told him I was going back to the hospital to demand another test, which I did.

The gynaecologist again told me that there was no chance I could be pregnant, but reluctantly booked me in for a scan.

Finally, I was proved right. The scan clearly showed a baby in my womb—I was five months pregnant. This was a total shock to everybody except me: the gynaecologist was amazed, and Kenn felt terrible for doubting me. But these kinds of miracles happen every day to people all over the world, and I was overjoyed that throughout I had listened to spirit and kept my faith.

I went into labour on my birthday, 8th June 1984. Kenn and I had gone into town to celebrate with Mathew, who was almost five.

Just as we were tucking into our steak at lunchtime, I began having contractions. Kenn took Mathew home while I went into hospital alone, and was in labour until dinner-time the next day. Finally, Elizabeth was born at 5:05 p.m. on Saturday 9th June. She had jet-black hair and looked so much bigger than Mathew at a healthy eight pounds.

I remember Kenn holding her in his arms and bursting into tears.

"We have to name her after Betty," he told me as he gazed into her eyes.

I smiled, feeling Betty's presence in the room. Betty's full name was Elizabeth Jane Benson. "Yes," I agreed. "I think your Gran had already decided that!" And so it was.

The next day, my daughter and I joined Kenn and Mathew at home. It was Father's Day, and Kenn was over-joyed with our family's new addition.

I returned to work two nights a week when Elizabeth was a couple of months old. A few weeks later, she developed a cold. I wasn't worried, but brought her cot into my and Kenn's bedroom to keep a closer eye on her. In the middle of the night I was woken by a sudden, strong pressure on my body—I thought our dog, Sam, had jumped up on to the bed, but when I sat up the pressure was gone and Sam wasn't in the room.

Confused, I glanced quickly around the room for any sign of spirit. I was just about to send out a thought, knowing there must be a message for me, when Dad's voice came through, strong and clear, his tone urgent: "*Check on Elizabeth!*"

Diving out of bed, I rushed to my daughter's cot. Elizabeth was breathing, but unconscious. I screamed at Kenn to wake up and tried to stay calm, clearing her airways while Kenn rushed downstairs to call the ambulance. At the hospital, my worst fears were confirmed: I was told that if I hadn't woken up and checked on Lizzy, she wouldn't have made it through the night.

Shortly afterward, I went to the spiritualist church with Kenn's Aunt Hilary—his father's sister.

It wasn't the church I usually attended, but we'd heard there was a good medium speaking that night and decided to go along. Unfortunately, that medium never showed up, so we decided to hold an open circle.

Open circles involve participation from everyone present, based on the idea that we all have a sixth sense we can tune in to. They vary from place to place, but more often than not the lights are dimmed, people sit in a circle in a relaxing room, and after prayers or meditation, speak about images or thoughts that are coming to them.

At the time, I didn't know much about this and wasn't expecting anything worth listening to, but it turned out to be an important turning point in my life.

One lady present looked very much like the gypsy lady I had met in Bradford all those years ago.

She cleared her throat and looked directly at me.

"I can see a small lady in spirit," she began. "It's a message for you."

The room was silent as we all waited for her to continue.

"This lady does an awful lot of work with you. She is very happy you named your daughter after her—Elizabeth, I think it is."

I nodded. "Yes," I said. "I do know who that is."

"I can see a man, too," she went on. "He's not in spirit. He loves you very much."

I thought of Kenn. "Yes," I repeated.

"It's not your husband."

I frowned, and Hilary turned and looked at me accusingly.

"There's only my husband," I told the lady. "I think this message is for someone else."

She paused and shook her head slowly.

"No … it's definitely for you," she told me. "Perhaps you're not aware of him yet. But you will be soon."

I was confused, and slightly annoyed that the message had been given in front of all these people, and in particular Hilary, who was extremely close to Kenn.

"So what was all that about?" Hilary demanded as we left the church.

"I have absolutely no idea," I told her.

"Well, *is* there anyone else in your life?" she asked.

"Not at all!" I replied. "And I have no intention of there being, either."

Hilary studied me as we walked along.

"Hmmm," she said. "Well, just you be careful."

"I'm very happy in my marriage, Hilary," I sighed. "Don't you worry about that."

Still, the message played on my mind for the next few days. Hilary knew Kenn and I had had problems over the episode with Kay, but I was telling the truth when I said I was happy: We had managed to put that night behind us and made a fresh start: we had been left some money in a will, the children were happy and healthy, and we had recently moved into a lovely new house.

But the gypsy lady had been so specific with Betty's message that I had problems brushing the rest of her prediction aside. I was so scared it might be true that I was reluctant to ask spirit myself, but a few months later curiosity overcame me and I decided to hold another séance with my friend Velma.

"Betty, could you tell us more about the message I was given at the spiritualist church?" I asked.

"*Yes*," she replied. "*There is indeed a man who will love you deeply. He will make himself known to you soon.*"

I shuddered.

"*This man has the initials R.P.*" Betty continued. "*They will mean a lot to you within the next year. He has connections to someone with exotic heritage. That's about all I need to tell you for now.*"

The séance continued with Betty giving Velma some very accurate messages, although I have to admit I wasn't really listening.

Who was this man? Where would we meet? Would I feel the same, and if I did, what kind of turmoil would that bring to my family? How should I handle things? And who around him would have exotic heritage? I went to bed that night feeling very anxious and scared.

When I next spoke to Betty, she told me that this man was coming closer and closer.

"*One day you will give birth to this man's son,*" she told me. "*Again, that's all I can tell you for now. But look out for him; it will all become clear quite soon.*"

I nearly fell off my chair with shock. I had never had reason to doubt Betty—in fact she had only ever proven herself a reliable source, but still—a son? To another man? It just didn't add up; it seemed ridiculous.

I wracked my brains for reasons as to why I would ever leave my husband and hurt my children by having an affair, but then it occurred to me that things might not be so black and white. What if I was only supposed to help this man? Perhaps I would be a surrogate? Perhaps he might not have a family, and our paths were destined to cross for that reason, and that reason only.

Although I felt very apprehensive and nervous about the future, part of me felt happy, excited. I had always known I would have another boy, but Kenn had decided after Elizabeth that he wanted a vasectomy. I was devastated about this, and had spent many a sleepless night wondering how on earth I would bring another child into the world when my husband was now infertile.

Over the next couple of days, Velma and I discussed the messages endlessly, trying to understand how things might pan out. We walked down to the local market to do some shopping and stopped at a café for a bite to eat.

While there, I bumped into Dave, an old friend of mine who was a nurse while I was a cadet. He was having lunch with several other workmen and told me he now worked as a builder. Dave and I chatted for a while as his friends talked amongst themselves, but there was another man present who I couldn't help but notice: he seemed a lot quieter than the others, and gave me a shy smile every time I caught his eye.

I told Dave that I'd just moved house and needed someone to build a wall outside.

"Would you be able to come and give me a quote?" I asked.

"No worries," Dave told me, getting out his diary. "I'll come with my boss next Tuesday if you like, 12:30 p.m.?"

A week later while Velma was at my house, a van pulled up outside.

"Right on time," I noted, feeding Elizabeth another spoonful of baby food.

Velma glanced out of the window and gasped loudly.

"What is it?" I asked, jumping up from my chair.

"My God," she exclaimed. "Look at the van, Bridget!"

My heart stopped. Written on the van were the words "Ron Paul Building Contractors."

"*R.P.,*" I croaked.

Velma took a sharp breath as a workman jumped out of the van with Dave. "He was at the café the other day," she whispered. "He's the one who smiled at you."

I was shaking like a leaf as I opened the door for them.

Ron came inside and shook my hand firmly.

"Would you like a coffee?" I asked nervously.

"No thanks, I can't stay," he smiled. "My son's in the car."

I looked and saw a dark-skinned boy waiting in the passenger seat. Odd … Ron was Caucasian, but at the time I thought nothing of it.

Ron measured up and promised me he would send a quote, but I never got it. His excuse was that it would cost me too much money, so Velma's son built the wall in the end.

Months went by and I was on my way to the shops when I noticed Ron working on a nearby house. He grinned and jumped down from the scaffolding to come and say hello. Elizabeth was gurgling in her pushchair and he bent down to coo at her.

"Isn't she beautiful?" Ron commented. She certainly was: brown curly hair and big green eyes. "I'd have loved to have had my own children," Ron confided.

I thought about the prediction and couldn't help myself.

"Don't worry," I told him with a glint in my eye. "One day I'll have your son."

Ron looked at me, frowning, trying to work out whether I was joking. My face was deadly serious. "You're stark raving bonkers," he told me bluntly, and shaking his head, he turned and walked back to the house.

I didn't feel embarrassed; my mind was ticking over about his first comment. He'd love to have children? Wasn't his son in the van the day he came to do an estimate?

Then I realised his son, Jason, who was very dark-skinned, must not be Ron's biological child. *Connections to someone with exotic heritage.* Everything started to fit into place.

Two years later in early 1987, we moved house again and I began to see Ron regularly: too regularly for it to be coincidence. Around this time, I began giving readings twice a day when I had a chance. It was more of a way to develop my gift and help people than a professional venture, but I enjoyed it so much I knew that at some point it would become a full-time calling—just as Dad and Harry had always told me.

One day, an elderly lady had called to the house with an unexpected gift. Her name was Pat Batty and she was an acquaintance from the spiritualist church.

"I have something for you," Pat told me.

She produced a beautiful crystal ball. "It's over four hundred years old," she explained. "It's been passed down through my family, but I'm afraid I can't make much use of it and would prefer it to go to someone who can."

I was bowled over at her generosity and accepted her kind present. She passed over shortly afterward, and I had always intended on keeping my promise to use it well.

I had never owned a crystal ball before but felt it was worth experimenting with, although I have to say I was very skeptical about its uses.

My friend June offered to make a pouch for the crystal ball; I have never been very good at sewing! She took it away and I thanked her and agreed to pick it up a few days later from her parents' house. It was her mother's birthday and I'd been invited to join the celebrations.

When I arrived, I was dismayed to see June pass the crystal ball to her mother. It's very bad practice to allow anyone to hold your ball, tarot cards, or anything else, unless conducting a reading.

But when June's mother handed the ball over to me, I almost fell over with shock. One look at the crystal ball showed me the unmistakable image of June's father, Max—who was sitting on the sofa next to me—lying in a coffin, pale and motionless. The shocking image was accompanied by a message from his late mother: "*It's his heart, you must tell him.*" This hit me like a ton of bricks: I should never have been skeptical about the ball.

Shaken, I turned to June's father, who had only just retired that week.

"Max, have you had any chest pain lately?"

He frowned and nodded slowly. "Well yes, I have, as a matter of fact," he replied.

I urged him to go to the doctors, but I knew that my advice was pointless: once I have seen death there is usually little hope. When it's your time, it's your time—I can convey a message, but I can't change what is inevitable. It's also morally wrong for me to terrify the wits out of people by telling them I can see a sudden death, so the worst kind of information has to be handled with care and compassion. However, I'm also a firm believer that miracles do happen, so I always ensure I tell people to get checked out if it seems to be something that could be treated by a doctor. Occasionally, something is found that could save a life.

We left and June asked me what I'd seen. When I told her, she was insistent I'd got it wrong. "My uncle Ronnie's not well," she told me. "I think it was probably him you're seeing."

But I knew I was right. A week later June called to tell me her father had had a heart attack at the bus stop. I never doubted the crystal ball again, and it has shown me some very disturbing images over the years. Nowadays, I prefer to use it only for healing.

Time went by and in March 1990 we moved house for a third and final time, to Regent Place where I still live today. It was the house Kenn was born and raised in.

I hadn't seen Ron for a while, but immediately after moving in, he came to work across the road from our house. I asked him for another estimate and this time he agreed—but he never carried out the work himself; he always sent his men.

Things became rocky with Kenn at this time. He was now working as a chef at a different hospital, and he became distant and moody. I felt alone; he never seemed to want to be in my company and we didn't see much of each other with our different working patterns.

I began to tire of working nights and feeling like a single mother. There wasn't much time to sleep during the day and spend quality time with Mathew and Elizabeth.

One night whilst getting ready for another long night shift, I had a sudden premonition that made me stop dead in my tracks. I was given an image of two cars driving over a local bypass called Burdock Way. One car was running the other off the road and I had a horrible knowledge that there would be a fatal accident, although the images stopped just before the collision.

I mentioned the premonition to my colleagues when I got to work. They could see how shaken I was and placed a lot of trust in my gift, but we were very busy so it wasn't discussed at length.

Still feeling anxious about the message, I went about my duties for an hour or so when the night sister's pager went off. She was called to the casualty department: there had indeed been an accident on Burdock Way. A car had spun out of control and had been impaled on a railing, killing a lady, a mother of two children, instantly.

I felt sick thinking about the young children this poor woman had left behind, and began to question my own priorities in life. Should I give up nursing and make my living from being a clairvoyant medium? At least I could put my young children first and balance my work life around their needs. After a few days' thought, I decided to go for it. I had been giving readings for three years now in my spare time and found that the messages came naturally, so I didn't feel at all nervous about a career change. I'd never needed to advertise, either—it was all word of mouth, but I had built up quite a client base this way and worked out there was enough interest for me to give ten to twelve readings a day.

And so it was that the poor lady's accident was instrumental in my decision to leave nursing and spend more time with my children. I handed my notice in immediately, and began my new life as a full-time clairvoyant medium in June 1990.

Shortly afterward, deep in my heart I felt a change toward Kenn. Although I'd expected our marriage to improve if I was at home more often, being at home with the children and making my money from readings made me feel independent. I didn't need Kenn anymore, and he continued to grow more and more distant from me.

CHAPTER 13

One night in December 1990, I had been writing a poem—a rather depressing verse about how trapped, lonely, and confused I felt in my life.

Kenn came home drunk after a night with friends in the pub. He snatched the piece of paper from me and I let him read it, hardly caring what he thought any more.

"You've got someone else, haven't you?" He shouted.

"No, I haven't," I replied quietly. "But I don't love you anymore."

"You're in love with that builder, aren't you?" Kenn sneered.

I didn't respond. Kenn stormed out of the room and left me sadly contemplating what the future held.

The next day, Kenn went to visit Ron at his office. Ron wasn't there, but unfortunately his wife, Linda, was. Kenn insisted on waiting for Ron to return, and when he did, Kenn demanded answers.

"What the hell is going on with you and my wife?"

"Nothing's going on," Ron told him. "We're just friends, but I will tell you this: I'll support her whatever happens with you two."

After a heated discussion, the details of which were never discussed in depth, Kenn left and Ron was forced to explain our relationship to his wife. Not that there was much to explain: at this point, it was as though all three of us had an inkling of the future, but nothing more than intuition and my spirit messages to base it on.

Kenn and I struggled to keep our relationship going, but things continued to deteriorate between us.

On 28th December—Kenn's only day off that week—I was due to go into hospital with fibroid problems. Fortunately, the appointment was put back until New Year's Eve. I was relieved and thought we could spend the day as a family; God knew we needed the quality time.

But Kenn had other ideas. He asked if I minded him going out with some friends, but he never came home.

I was furious, and called all the pubs in our area demanding to know if anyone had seen my husband. I had no luck and got in the car, strapping the kids in the back and setting out to find him. When I did, he was in the pub, gambling.

We had no money; I saw red and slapped him across the face. "You can stay with your cronies, don't bother coming home," I screamed before storming out.

He didn't come home. I went into hospital on New Year's Eve and Kenn wasn't there to take me or pick me up. I knew instinctively there was another woman in his life. A few days after coming out of hospital, I asked Betty if my worst fears were correct.

"*The initials are J.B.,*" she confirmed. "*You'll find proof in his wallet, but don't do it now.*"

Shaking, I attempted to act normally as I got ready to go to the spiritualist church, but decided at the last minute not to go. Kenn was in the bath, and I knew it was now or never to find out why our marriage was in such trouble.

I took the opportunity to look through his jeans pockets and retrieved his wallet. There were three numbers, which I wrote down, my heart pounding, feeling sick. I replaced the numbers and struggled to remain chirpy with him that evening.

The next day I picked up the telephone.

One was the number of a pub near the hospital where he worked. The second, I gathered from an answering machine message that made my stomach churn, was his mistresses' marital home. The third turned out to be the number of the house his girlfriend had intended for Kenn to eventually share with her. I knew instinctively this was the number where I would get hold of her, and I called obsessively until it was answered.

Eventually, a woman picked up.

"Who's this?" I asked, shakily.

"I could ask the same question," came the reply.

"Are you Janet?" I asked, after a prompt in my ear from Betty.

A pause.

"Yes, I am. Who's this?"

I took a deep breath.

"I'm Kenn's wife," I told her. Then I gained courage. "What the hell are your numbers doing in my husband's wallet?"

I was met by a torrent of abuse, swearing, shouting.

"It's nothing to do with you," she told me aggressively. "You don't deserve Kenn, you never did."

I gasped at her tone. How *dare* she?

"We're together now," Janet said stiffly. "Leave us alone and get on with your own life."

She slammed down the phone and left me shaking with fury and sadness. My world had been turned upside down.

Only seconds later, Kenn came home from work and I flew at him in anger.

"I know what you're up to," I screeched, hitting and punching him in my rage.

"I've spoken to your fancy woman, she thinks you're together now! How *could* you? You've made a fool of me!"

Kenn never defended himself or argued with me, he never even tried to explain or comfort me. This just made me angrier.

"Get out of this house," I screamed, launching things across the room. "Pack your bags and go and live in your love nest!"

He did as he was told. Luckily the children were playing outside and didn't hear a thing. Kenn left quietly, and it was down to me to explain as best I could that Mummy and Daddy were separating.

"Whatever happens, he will still be your dad and you'll still see him all the time," I told them, struggling to keep my voice steady. "He loves you very much but he doesn't love me anymore."

Mathew, now twelve, started to cry. He'd always felt so lucky that his Mum and Dad were together in a time when so many of his friends' parents were divorced, and he said he'd thought his family was happy and would stay together forever. It was heartbreaking.

At seven, Elizabeth was too young to understand fully, but she sensed the atmosphere and saw her big brother in tears, so she was inconsolable too. It was one of the hardest days of my life.

When I told my mother that Kenn and I were splitting up, she was also very distressed.

"You've brought shame on the family," she shouted tearfully.

"It's this work of yours, you're possessed!"

Mum even spoke to the parish priest, asking him to come and bless me. He did so, but in my own grief I refused to see him.

Not long after, Ron's wife came for a reading. I knew in advance I'd be facing her, and knew that she was aware of me—especially after Kenn's outburst in the office a few weeks earlier. It didn't make any sense why she would come to see me. I racked my brains, but couldn't fathom it out.

Perhaps she wanted to see me up close, get a better picture of who I was. Perhaps she hoped we'd have a chance to discuss the strange situation we were a part of, or maybe she thought I'd be obliged to tell her if there was anything on the cards about Ron and myself—a great way for her to do some detective work.

But although I was apprehensive about what would come out, and Linda's reasons for the visit, I never mentioned anything to Ron at the time; privacy and confidentiality are very important in my line of work.

On the day, feeling nervous and still wondering why on earth Linda would choose to see me of all people, I eventually settled into the reading. The first thing I saw was that Linda was having an affair—and she was looking for guidance as to whether she should leave Ron. Linda strongly denied this when I relayed the information, but it turned out to be true. It wasn't her first affair, either—Jason was never fathered by Ron (something they were both aware of with the differences in skin tone, of course).

The reading continued and I gave her more messages on other areas of her life, before seeing something that stopped me dead: Ron was to have another child. With me.

It's definitely true.

I didn't tell Linda this.

When I next spoke to Ron, I poured out my heart about Kenn's affair. He told me he knew how I felt; he and Linda were splitting up too.

"Can I take you out?" he asked.

I was unsure, but thinking of Kenn with Janet, and knowing Ron was the only person in the world who understood what I was going through, I agreed.

Ron and I went out for a meal and a drink; that was as far as it went. We talked about how much our lives had changed over the past year, our betrayals, our hopes for the future, and I decided, tentatively, to tell him everything Betty had said.

Thankfully, he didn't call me crazy this time. We'd both been through so many ups and downs that nothing seemed impossible.

Kenn came to see the children every day, although I'd always leave the room while he was there. Once a week, I went out with Ron. It was only ever for a couple of hours, and Kenn and I never spoke about it. As soon as I got home, Kenn would leave.

It was surreal to be dating Ron. I felt that I had to, for reasons beyond my understanding, but my vows were still important to me. The whole time I was seeing him, I was in turmoil.

This was not the life I had chosen! I wanted a happy marriage, children with my husband, love that lasted forever. But Ron made me feel safe, special. I knew he cared for me deeply, and never once did he try to take advantage of my vulnerability.

Ron and I did discuss the possibility of me having his son.

"I believe Betty, but deep down I don't know how it could ever work out," I confided.

Ron nodded slowly.

"Do you want another child?" He asked. "With me?"

I sighed.

"Nothing would make me happier than a new baby," I told him. "But I have no intention of hurting my children or starting a relationship."

Ron agreed. "I understand," he told me. "But I have to admit, after thinking a lot about what Betty predicted, the idea of being a dad ... well, I'd like it too. But at the same time all this has turned everything upside down. It's pretty overwhelming."

We were both confused, and continued dating with no sexual relationship in sight. But that conversation had made things seem possible somehow. The fact was, I wanted another child. Kenn, already infertile, had left, and my polycystic ovaries meant that the chances of another child were already slim. It was now or never.

I told Kenn what Betty had said—that spirit told me I would have Ron's child, but there would be no relationship with him. Kenn didn't react, but he did sit the children down and tell them I was with another man. The fallout from this—heartbroken children and constant arguments with Kenn—was too much to deal with, and in November 1991, I told Ron I couldn't continue seeing him.

I was confused and emotionally exhausted; I had no idea of my feelings anymore. I had a business to run, a home to keep, and two children who needed me: I had to control my emotions.

"I'm so sorry, Ron," I told him. "But I just don't know where it's going with us, and everything's getting out of hand. I can't bear seeing the kids so upset and angry. I can't do this anymore."

Ron didn't look surprised to hear this. We'd spoken of nothing else, and he'd already admitted the pressure was getting to him, too.

"It's fine," he said. "I totally understand. To be honest, I don't feel I'm in a position to support you and the kids … especially with the extra one we've talked about." He grinned. "No hard feelings."

What started as a simple goodbye became a hug, then a kiss, and Ron and I ended up sleeping together for the first and only time since this whole saga began. I'd never been with another man but Kenn, and I needed to know how it felt with Ron: would it feel right? Wrong? Indifferent?

I felt a mixture of emotions as I lay in his arms. Certainly, I wasn't surprised at myself. I had known for a long time that we would become more than friends eventually, although it seemed quite bizarre to cross that boundary on the night we said goodbye. I was glad it happened and I felt content, but at the same time I had no wish for it to happen again, no sadness at the thought our union was a one-off. Rather, everything felt simple now. As it should be, no more, no less. It was as though we had been pawns in some cosmic game of fate and destiny, and this was the endgame. It was out of our hands, and I knew I had to concentrate on the children and get on with my life as though it had never happened.

Three months later, in February 1992, my periods stopped.

I broke the news to Kenn first, and he was fantastic. Since I'd stopped seeing Ron, our relationship had become quite strong again. We were not only civil, but we were having fun together and enjoying each other's company more than ever. Sometimes he'd stay over after seeing the children, and although I presumed he was still seeing Janet, her name was never mentioned by either of us.

"I'll support you," Kenn told me, his eyes wide and solemn.

"I love you, and come hell or high water, I'll support you with this baby. I'll bring it up as my own, if you'll have me."

I was so relieved I could cry.

Unfortunately, the children were not so understanding about me having a baby with a man who wasn't their daddy. Mathew sat and wept while Elizabeth screamed and flew at me in a rage, punching me in the stomach. They had been through so much because of Kenn and I, so I couldn't blame them. Instead, I concentrated on positive thoughts, knowing they would love their little brother in time.

But when I went to get the pregnancy confirmed, I was told yet again that I wasn't carrying a child.

"It's impossible," my consultant said. "Mrs. Benson, at your age..." He glanced down at his notes... "At thirty-six years old, and with your gynaecological problems, I would actually advise that you undergo a hysterectomy."

"I'll do no such thing," I snapped. "I am pregnant, you just mark my words."

Another three months passed before I had a positive pregnancy test and Betty's prediction was confirmed. I was overjoyed but not at all surprised, and nervously, I broke the news to Ron.

"It's happened," I told him. "I'm six months pregnant with your son."

Ron's face broke into a huge grin and he threw his arms around me and squeezed me tight. "I knew it would happen," he laughed. "I knew it!"

I was relieved he was happy, and there was no bad feeling between any of us at all. Kenn and I were pretty much back together, Ron's wish to father his own child would be granted, and the children—well, I knew that we could repair the damage done now that we were back together as a family.

For the first time in a long time, looking forward to my special son's coming birth, I felt at peace.

❀ PART THREE ❀
Finding
Peace

CHAPTER

14

Marcus was born on the 3rd August 1992, on Kenn's mother's birthday. It would have felt wrong choosing between the two men in my life as my birthing partner, so I decided to have Kenn's Aunt Hilary there to hold my hand.

I had a difficult birth, resulting in a caesarian section, but I was able to hold Marcus immediately. Even as a newborn with yellow jaundice, he was bonny and smiley.

Kenn and the children visited at the hospital as soon as they got the message. My husband broke down as he tenderly held the new arrival, just as he had with Mathew and Elizabeth.

This time though, Kenn's tears were not only for Marcus. He was overwhelmed because it had finally hit him that all the predictions were true. We'd been married sixteen years, but during this time Kenn had still managed to maintain a healthy skepticism!

Now, holding Marcus, his doubts about the spirit world were no more.

Mathew and Elizabeth fell in love with their little brother at first sight; we were like any ordinary family gathered around the hospital bed.

As strange as it sounds, the matter of who would bring Marcus up was never discussed. It was as though fate had intervened to make this odd situation as simple as possible: we were all to play equal roles in his upbringing, and there has never been any drama about any of it.

However, Kenn and I hit another rocky patch when Marcus was almost seven months old. I had decided not to attend the spiritualist church one Sunday evening. I wasn't sure why, but intuition told me I needed to stay at home.

"Don't think I'll bother tonight," I told Kenn breezily.

A look of panic crossed his face.

I frowned.

"What's wrong?"

"Nothing," Kenn stammered.

Why is he so uneasy?

I knew then that he was expecting a call from Janet while I was out, but said nothing.

"Right, I'll go and get a bottle of wine if we're staying in together," Kenn said, grabbing his coat and heading out.

He was gone for quite a while.

"That's it," I muttered, picking up the phone and dialing Janet's home number. It was engaged and we had no mobiles in those days. When I finally got through a woman answered, but I didn't recognise the voice.

"It's like trying to get through to Buckingham Palace," I grumbled.

"Ah, that'll be because Janet's been on the phone to that Kenn," came the reply. I found out later it was her twin sister.

"I see," I muttered, my heart pounding. "Right, thank you for that.'"

I hung up and sat taking deep breaths, waiting for Kenn to return.

When he finally walked through the door, he had no wine.

"Sorry, no shops open," he said casually.

"You went out to call Janet, didn't you?" I said quietly.

Kenn's face fell.

"Don't be silly."

"I already know, Kenn," I told him, my voice rising. "I called that number and she was engaged because you were calling her from the phone box. Don't lie to me!"

We had a huge bust up and I asked him to leave again. This time he stayed with Hilary and didn't return to Janet's: despite me catching them out, Kenn had insisted they were no longer together.

I returned to Ireland with the children after Kenn left; I needed a holiday. Again, I had a difficult time explaining things to the children. I simply told them that Dad and I had been through a lot and needed some time apart to think, but that it would all be alright. They took it in their stride this time; they had adjusted well and they knew they still had the love and support of both parents and our families.

After returning home, I had some more bad news—a family friend had passed with cancer. Her name was Joanne.

I had previously nursed her, and had also given her a reading in which I saw her funeral. It was a tragic death—Joanne had only been married a few weeks before she passed and my heart went out to her new husband.

Kenn knew the family too, so when he offered me a lift to the funeral I accepted.

But the day before the service, I saw an image of a crash involving a red car and white car in an area of Halifax that was known to me, and I instinctively knew it was another premonition: this time meant for me.

On the day of the funeral, I felt very apprehensive, but went through with my plans because there didn't seem a good enough reason not to. I wanted to pay my respects, and besides, there was no reason for us to go anywhere near the area I'd seen in the images.

I got into our red car with Marcus and Kenn, feeling nervous but telling myself our route was safe. Mathew and Elizabeth were staying behind at school. We went to the funeral, did some shopping, and got back into the car to pick the children up.

As we rounded a corner on our way home, I saw that a policeman was directing traffic away from the route we had planned on taking—the road had been closed. I realised with horror that instead, we would have to pass through the area I had seen in my premonition.

"*Brace yourself,*" I heard my father's voice suddenly, and then immediately afterwards—just as it had been in my mind's eye—a white car pulled out of a side road and smashed straight into the driver's side of our car.

Marcus was in a car seat in the front and I was sitting behind him; Kenn swerved and took the worst of the impact. It broke a bone in his shoulder and the steering wheel went straight into his stomach. Both cars were write-offs.

The driver of the other car was a woman, who, to my horror, drove away from the scene. She then stopped farther down the street. I'm not sure what was going on in her mind, but she marched over to our car and put a note on our windscreen with her insurance details—she never said a word. Kenn was screaming and shouting at her, but I think she must have been in shock. The lady walked silently back to her car and stayed inside until the police turned up.

I was amazed how nobody stopped to help, even though I was holding Marcus in my arms and he was clearly traumatised. Then, in a strange twist of fate, I saw Ron driving down the street towards our wrecked vehicle.

"What happened?" he asked frantically, jumping out of the van and running toward us. "I was driving the other way and something told me to come back."

I explained, between sobs and Marcus's screams, how the crash had happened. Kenn didn't look happy with Ron's appearance, but the gravity of the situation forced him to swallow his pride. He asked Ron to take Marcus and myself to the hospital to get checked over while he waited for the police.

I was given a sling without an X-ray, and only discovered the following day that I had fractured my shoulder. I also had bruising on my chest, but luckily Marcus was fine.

Kenn never went to the doctors or hospital, and to this day still suffers.

But the accident made Kenn and I realise how much we meant to each other. He had no car and no means of getting to work from his Aunt Hilary's, so he came back home. A colleague lived opposite and had offered to take him to work every day.

It seemed normal that Kenn was back in the marital home, and I have always felt the accident needed to happen to repair our damaged marriage. It made me feel lucky to be alive, to appreciate my beautiful family. The thought that Mathew and Elizabeth could have been left all alone that day terrified me.

It must have changed something because Kenn and I haven't had any problems since.

Over the years, things have fallen into place and my relationship with both men is clear-cut: Kenn is my husband and Ron is the father of my youngest son. I don't make a big fuss telling people Marcus has a different Dad; to us it's perfectly normal. I'm sure some people don't understand and I have occasionally felt judged, but it works for us so I've never been bothered by any gossip.

Marcus has two fathers and he loves them both. He often tells me that when he graduates from university he'll have both Kenn and Ron at his side, while Mathew and Elizabeth respect Ron and there are no problems.

Marcus was immediately accepted by Kenn's family, and even my mother, who hadn't been at all happy while I was pregnant, came around soon after he was born. She has always had a soft spot for him as her youngest grandchild.

So, as I was told all those years before by the gypsies in Bradford, I now have my daughter and my two boys.

Mathew is now thirty-one and, as predicted, is a good musician and a fantastic artist. He studied architecture at Glasgow University and is now fully qualified and doing very well for himself. He lives in the same village with his partner, Rachel, and I'm very proud of him.

Elizabeth is now twenty-six and, as predicted, is a nursery nurse with a fantastic gift for dealing with children. She is kind and loving and a fantastic mother to my first grandchild, Lennon. She lives right next door to Kenn and I with her partner, Matt.

And then there's Marcus, now eighteen. As predicted, he excels at music, art, and all kinds of sports. He's a keen swimmer, diver, cricketer, and rugby player, and is still living at home, studying for his A levels.

Mathew is quite reserved, private, and sensible. Marcus is much more emotional and open, but just as levelheaded. Of all the children, it is Elizabeth who has caused me the most strife! She is passionate, fiery, and rebellious, and was a difficult adolescent: she's come home with a pierced tongue and tattoos and kept me awake worrying when she's been out until all hours in the morning. But thankfully it was just a normal teenage phase, and our relationship is very strong now that she's an adult with a child of her own.

I told Elizabeth about her twin brother as soon as she was able to understand, and I always felt he was around her as she grew up. This was confirmed at the spiritualist church when she was eleven. We had gone along together and Lizzy was given a message; the medium played Michael Jackson's "Ben" and told us that Charles Daniel had come to her before the service, letting the speaker know his twin sister would be there that night.

Elizabeth was in floods of tears, as was I. It might seem strange that I don't communicate with Charles myself, but to me it makes perfect sense. It's always been as though he's there for Elizabeth rather than me. I think of him every year on Elizabeth's birthday and wonder what he looks like as an adult in spirit—but I'm not sure I could cope emotionally if I connected with Charles. He is where he was meant to be, and I just thank God he looks after my daughter.

CHAPTER 15

Over the years, I have given hope to many people by proving there is another world beyond this mortal coil, and our loved ones are just a thought away. But there have also been those harrowing experiences that make my job extremely distressing at times.

I was deeply affected by a murder case in November 1994, where a thirteen-year-old girl from a small and close-knit community vanished after a trip to a local shop one night.

The case attracted national media attention, and numerous people were questioned over her disappearance as miles of canals in the local area were trawled by divers looking for the girl's body.

One night soon after she went missing, spirit showed me the stretch of canal where the girl's body lay hidden. Images flashed in my mind of the events leading up to her death: an argument, somebody strangling her, the frantic transportation of the poor girl to the nearby canal in the early hours of the morning, where her limp body was weighed down with bricks. Spirit told me that she wasn't dead before she hit the water, only unconscious, although this was never confirmed.

Although divers had already searched this stretch of water, I was convinced that the disturbing images I had seen were real. I contacted an old friend who now works for the Criminal Investigation Department, and she took me to the police station. The officer in charge of the case looked at me as though I was crazy, and it was never followed up. I was beside myself. I couldn't sleep or eat because of the terrifying images and the exasperation of not being heard.

In April 1995, the girl's body was finally recovered by canal workers in the very same spot I had seen. Sure enough, her body had been weighed down with bricks, and the autopsy report stated there were signs of strangulation.

By 2004, more than five thousand people had been spoken to and hundreds of witness statements had been taken, but no one has ever been charged over the murder. It's a tragic crime which is still fresh in the minds of everyone in the community sixteen years later.

It is very difficult not to lose faith when these kinds of things happen. Generally the system is run in such a way that clairvoyance has no place in a crime investigation, and to say I felt frustrated by the police's attitude to my work would be a huge understatement—especially as I'm sure I know who murdered that poor child. But I like to think that this is improving as society becomes more spiritual and open to the idea that we all have a sixth sense, and when this sense is developed, as mine is, it's just as valid and real as touch, taste, or sight.

In my work, crimes quite often emerge from readings I've given. A few years ago, a lady came to me and I instantly knew that her ex-husband was hiding a particularly nasty secret. I saw that he was sexually abusing his two children and broached the subject with the lady, who broke down. It turned out she'd had her suspicions for a long time but had no evidence to support her intuition.

I asked to see the daughter, now a troubled teenager, and coaxed her to tell a teacher or professional. The poor girl cried with relief that somebody finally knew, and did as I'd advised. The case is now going to court and I am hopeful that I have been instrumental in serving justice for this man through my work.

Sometimes, cases are so notorious I'm in shock when the messages come to pass. One such example is the tragic death of Princess Diana.

In life, Betty was traditional in her views and loved talking about the royal family. This didn't end after she passed, and she continued chatting to me about what was going on in the lives of the English monarchs.

In 1990 her messages on this subject became more regular. She told me that Princess Diana and Prince Charles would divorce, and that in 1997 Diana's life would come to a tragic end. I can't go into details of the messages too much for legal reasons, but I don't believe the car crash was an accident: let's just say Betty's messages (even years before the Princess's demise) mirror some of the so-called conspiracy theories we've all read about in the press since Diana passed over.

The catastrophic events of 9/11 are another such example.

In 2000, I went to work in New York for six weeks. I loved the Big Apple—the people, the food, the hustle and bustle of city life. I could have stayed there for good if it wasn't for the foreboding feeling I had deep in my stomach, the same feeling I'd had so many times, that knot of unease and apprehension. I just couldn't put my finger on it, but as the days passed I became desperate to get back to the U.K. where I was safe.

One day toward the end of my trip, I was taking a break and doing some sightseeing. I rounded a corner and came into sight of the Twin Towers, and instantly my uneasy feeling intensified. "What am I feeling?" I asked my guides.

"*By next year, those buildings will have gone*," Betty answered. "*Planes will hit them and everything will change: it will have enormous repercussions around the world for many years.*"

Her words did nothing to dispel my nervousness as you can imagine, but after years of doing this work I know that when I ask, I receive. I saw an image of the falling buildings, eaten up by fire, and heard screams and sirens. Then as quickly as it came, it was gone.

On my return I got in touch with my police contact once more, in the hope she could do something to prevent the attack by liaising with U.S. intelligence. Like many clairvoyant mediums across the globe who foresaw 9/11, my concerns were ignored. It is a sad mark of our society that we continue to brush away the importance of a sixth sense simply because it cannot be proven in scientific tests, and unfortunately intuition is a useless tool when the authorities refuse to take it seriously. All I can do is keep my conscience clear by reporting what I feel at the time, and hoping it is acted upon.

When the planes hit the Twin Towers a year later, I was devastated that I had not been able to stop the terrible event. I was overcome with grief for the people who perished and the families they had left behind, but was forced to get on with my life as though the horrendous premonition had never happened.

The infamous October 2000 train crash at Hatfield in Hertfordshire, England, was yet another illustration of this—terrifying images of forthcoming disasters are an occupational hazard for me.

A train leaving London for Leeds derailed just thirteen minutes after leaving King's Cross station, badly injuring seventy and killing four of the one hundred and seventy passengers on board. Unfortunately this time, two of the men who lost their lives in the horrific accident were known to me.

Both men were employed by Lucinda, a close friend of mine. She had come to me for a reading the week before, and while we were chatting about other areas of her life I was given the message that there would be a huge train crash the following Tuesday. Out of respect for their families, I can't name the men who passed that day, and some details have been changed to protect the identities of those involved.

Lucinda lives with the rest of her extended family on an island off the British coast. She was in Leeds to bring home her sister Caroline, who was recovering from an operation in a local hospital and due to go home on the Tuesday. Lucinda's plan was to collect Caroline and then leave by plane that day; her employees would be meeting her in Leeds to travel home with Caroline and herself.

"Please Lucinda, please don't travel on Tuesday," I begged her. "You must leave it a day later, and whatever you do, don't ask your staff to catch a train up here to meet you."

Lucinda was in a dilemma about what to do for the best, but the arrangements were out of her hands and she had no choice but to get back home on the day of the crash. So the plan went ahead—although she did pass the message on to the men involved, making me feel slightly better that my premonition had been discussed.

On the day it happened, Lucinda received a voicemail from one of the men who was to perish just a few hours later. He told her he intended to catch the 12:40 p.m. train from London to Leeds. Then she had another, this time saying he had changed his mind and would be getting an earlier train, the 12:10 p.m. Great North Eastern Express, with his colleague.

Lucinda had a bad feeling that this was the train I had seen in the crash, and in her frantic rush to call her employee back, she accidentally deleted his messages and was unable to get hold of him.

Both men died that day. Lucinda was devastated, as was I.

The strangest thing was that several weeks before the crash, I had accompanied Caroline to the clinic before she went in for her operation. On the way home, I was ravenous and suggested we stop somewhere for lunch. For one reason or another, Caroline decided she didn't like the look of every pub we passed, until eventually I couldn't wait for food any longer and persuaded her to get some food in a country inn near Halifax.

We walked in and were met by a busy crowd, all dressed very smartly.

"Can I help you?" A lady asked, coming over to us with a quizzical expression on her face.

"Yes please, we'd just like to see the menu," I replied.

The lady shook her head. "Sorry, but this is a funeral party," she told us softly.

Exactly the same thing happened while I was with Lucinda in the weeks running up to the train crash. It was as if spirit were preparing the three of us for the tragedy.

Then things got stranger. Three years after the Hatfield crash, I was with Marcus, visiting Lucinda on the island where she lives. It was the birthday of one of the men who were killed that day, and Lucinda and I went to the garden centre to buy some rose bushes in memory of that fateful day.

Standing at the checkout buying the plants—Lucinda at one till and me at the other—an elderly lady in front of

Lucinda, accompanied by another female, suddenly turned and smiled at me.

"*Hello.*"

I smiled back. "Hello."

"*How are you?*"

I racked my brains. She looked familiar …

"I'm fine," I said. "Do I … do I know you?"

"*Of course you know me,*" the lady laughed. "*Can I speak to you outside?*"

I nodded, still wondering where on earth I'd seen her before. "Yes, of course," I replied slowly.

Then I noticed the faces of the two girls behind the tills. They were exchanging smirks and glances, which instantly told me they couldn't see the lady. They thought I was crazy. I looked at Marcus, standing behind me with Lucinda's son John. The children's expressions signaled they couldn't see anything either.

I then looked at Lucinda, but my friend's pale face told a different story: her gaze was following the two women as they left the building.

We paid for our plants and took the children back to the car before meeting the two ladies at the trolley point. Both Lucinda and I were shivering from head to foot in their presence.

"*What's your name?*" The older lady asked me as we approached.

"Bridget."

"*Ahh,*" she smiled. "*My late mother's name was Bridget.*"

I waited apprehensively. Both Lucinda and the second spirit lady were silent.

"I need you to know that the man whose birthday it is today is fine and well," the lady began. At no point did she address Lucinda. *"He says that he needs his family to know that the crash was nobody's fault. It was simply a problem with the track."*

Then, as if someone had sprinkled dust over them and their bodies had become sand; she and her friend simply fell away from sight.

Lucinda was more shocked than I, having never had an experience quite like it, and the bizarre event was discussed on many occasions. I believe the spirit ladies made their presence known to Lucinda because she needed to hear it firsthand, in order to move on with her life.

It seems the mysterious lady was right—an investigation into the train accident put the cause of the crash down to over three hundred critical cracks in the railway line around Hatfield. Rail infrastructure employees were taken to court two years after the spirit lady's message at the garden centre, although all were acquitted for manslaughter.

As for who that spirit lady was, I still don't know. But I have a feeling I will see her again; the answers will come when they are meant to come.

I feel blessed to know that when my loved ones are in danger I will know about it and can hopefully prepare myself better, even if I'm too late to stop an impending disaster.

When Mathew was seventeen, he had a very serious car accident—it was a miracle he survived.

He was studying at college in the next town and had just passed his driving test, so I'd given him my car to use. On this particular day, he was late getting out of bed. I'd been shouting up the stairs and was quite annoyed by the time he got himself ready for college. We exchanged a few words and he stormed out of the house in a typically teenage fashion, while I muttered under my breath and got ready for my first appointment of the day.

After he had been gone about forty-five minutes, Dad suddenly interrupted my work.

"*Mathew has been in a car crash.*"

I stopped and looked at the lady to whom I was giving a reading.

"Mathew has been in a car crash," I repeated.

The lady frowned.

"Who's Mathew?'

Then it hit me.

"It's my son," I told her.

"*He's okay,*" Dad continued. "*But lucky to be alive.*"

I was very shaken, especially considering we had parted on bad terms. I finished work and heard my phone ringing in the next room. I rang the number back; it was a telephone box.

"Who's that?" I asked frantically.

"I'm just passing by and heard the phone ring," a man replied.

"I think my son's been trying to call," I said quickly. "Is there any sign of an accident anywhere nearby?"

"Yes, there has been an accident. The police are here," the man told me.

Because Mathew had no mobile phone at the time, I had no choice but to simply wait. It was less than an hour before the police car pulled up at the house, but it felt like an eternity. Mathew was with the officers, and although he was shaken and pale, there wasn't a scratch on him.

He'd been hit by a thirty-two-tonne arctic wagon, which had come straight across the roundabout into the path of his car. Mathew had been trapped inside as the vehicle overturned, and had been forced to kick open the passenger side door to escape from the wreck.

"Something really strange happened, Mum," Mathew confided after all the panic. "A man's voice came into my head … the voice told me to just hold on, so that's all I did."

I cried with relief. "That's Grandad," I told him.

Mathew's near-death experience made me vow that I would never again let any of my family leave the house on bad terms. I thank God that my loved ones in the spirit world stepped in that day—it isn't often people survive a crash like Mathew's.

People often ask me where home is, and I answer that I have two homes: I grew up in England and married an Englishman, so of course England means a lot to me. But I live my life through my Irish ancestry, and I am very proud of my Celtic roots.

In 2006 I met up with my oldest friends—Marion, Maureen, and Margaret. After Dad died, we'd moved to England in such a rush that I never got a chance to say goodbye to them. Seeing my classmates again was lovely, and although it had been thirty-eight years since we'd all been together in Mr. O'Shea's class, it was almost like we'd never parted.

But reconnecting with my Irish past only really began after I decided to work in Straide in 2002. I felt a sudden pull towards my homeland around this time and decided to rebuild relationships with my cousins Mary and Phina Knight after many years of lost contact. I also got back in touch with my old school friend Tom Howley, whose mother was buried in a joint funeral service with my Dad all those years before.

On one of these early visits to Straide in 2002, I stayed in a room at the Copper Beech pub. It's a very traditional Irish inn, painted with the colours of County Mayo—green, red, and yellow. The walls are adorned with photographs and quotes from local legend Michael Davitt, a Straide-born social campaigner who grew up during the Great Famine and went on to be one of Ireland's national treasures.

While staying in the pub that year, I decided to bite the bullet and advertise my readings in the local newspaper. It escalated from there, and within a few days I'd had that many calls I needed a receptionist to take my bookings!

Brian Gaughan, the licensee, introduced me to his sister Noreen, who offered to help out by answering the phone and keeping a diary for my Irish readings. From the minute we met, Noreen and I became great friends.

After finding people eager for readings, I had to stop working from my room above the Copper Beech—Noreen was taking so many bookings I decided I needed a more appropriate base while I was in Ireland. Marion Walsh, another old friend who used to sing with me in the choir when we were children, took me under her wing and offered to rent me an apartment in Straide. Like Noreen's family, Marion and her relations were caring and loving to me from the start, and gave me a warm and authentic Irish welcome.

After a year of travelling back and forth from England to Ireland, it was like I'd never left. My work was spread through word of mouth like wildfire, and I now go back to Straide six or seven times a year, for a week or so each time, to accommodate all the people who want to see me. I either stay at my friend Rita's empty cottage (she now lives in England), or at the apartment I rent from her sister Marion. Both of these are homely, tranquil places in which to give readings and enjoy my time in Ireland.

People always know I'm back in Straide; news travels fast in small Irish villages. They are warm people, and there's always a hearty welcome awaiting. If there's a party, you're invited. I love the fact that in Ireland, family values are as strong as ever, and I love the traditional sense of community and togetherness.

The downside is that I'm a subject for gossip and some people want to know what my business is there. A few have been quite vocal, objecting to my presence and my work after a few drinks, but I tend to ignore that. Generally though, I've been welcomed in with open arms. I still sing in church (and up on stage in the Copper Beech!) and people recognize me and know my work.

One memorable message I gave a couple of years ago was to a man propping up the bar in the Copper Beech one lunchtime. I was tucking into a cola and a sandwich when I found myself drawn to him: I knew instinctively he had given up on life.

The man was drunk, and spirit told me he'd been that way for many a year. He seemed surprised when I approached him and said hello.

"You're not very happy, are you?" I asked him softly.

He was taken aback, but images started flowing into my mind one after another—a child, an illness, an affair, a betrayal, a death … it turned out his ex-wife had given birth to a little boy some twenty years before, and the man had been overjoyed, despite the boy having a severe disability. But it turned out the boy wasn't his. This grief was compounded by his wife leaving him, and shortly after that the little boy passed to spirit. Heartbroken and inconsolable, the man turned to drink. He hadn't been sober since.

I explained my work, then gently told him what I saw. Tears poured down his cheeks as he confirmed my message was true, and he thanked me over and over for talking to him. I don't know whether it was too late to save that poor soul, but I felt that I had given him a lifeline and I hope it was an important turning point for him to face his grief at last.

Another time, my friend Ann—Noreen's sister—was having trouble conceiving. She had two lovely boys but was desperate for another baby. Ann had been trying for six years, only to discover her fallopian tubes were blocked. I sent out some healing thoughts and asked spirit for help, and almost immediately she fell pregnant and was over the moon. Ann had a baby girl, followed soon after by another boy, and she considers them little miracles—it just goes to show we can ask spirit for help with anything!

In February 2007 I was asked to do an audience at the Royal Theatre in Castlebar near Straide, and appeared again in July the same year.

The first in particular was very memorable and a roaring success—my children came to watch and were as amazed as me to see the queues of people waiting for my autograph after the show!

My father was working with me that night, in front of a full house. For my very first message, Dad drew my attention to an elderly woman who sat in the front row.

"*Go to the lady in the red coat,*" he told me.

I gave her a message from her late husband, who was berating her for not taking her medication.

Just as I was leaving her, she piped up: "I knew your father, you know. He used to talk about you all the time when you were a little girl."

I gasped and nearly dropped my microphone. I heard Dad chuckle.

"He was a very gifted man," she told me. "Very spiritual, like you."

As I thanked her, my eyes welled with tears and I was afraid I'd lose it on stage. It felt like the message was Dad's gift to me, and I was extremely moved. It was a fantastic start to a successful evening. It's always nerve-wracking standing in front of so many people and relying entirely on spirit, but my confidence grew after the lady's moving words and the night went off with a bang, Dad helping me every step of the way.

Generally, though, Irish people are much more private than the English, so I don't tend to do many audiences in Ireland. Because Irish society is built upon Catholicism, religion is strongly reflected in the norms and values of the people. This shows itself in a deep sense of privacy; a general attitude of not wanting to air one's dirty laundry in public, and as a result Irish clients prefer to see me in confidence rather than having their business shouted out in a theatre hall.

In contrast, I have held many audiences in England. My first ever was at the Civic Theatre in Halifax in 1992, where I raised funds for the children's ward at Leeds Hospital. I did so again in 1993, both times appearing in front of a full house.

It was a very rewarding experience, but also extremely emotional knowing that no matter how much money I raised, I wouldn't be able to save some of the children who were desperately fighting for life.

But in 2004, I was honoured to be asked to a fundraising event in Jersey for the Great Ormond Street Hospital. It's a very well-known and special place for sick children from all over the world, so I was moved to have been able to offer my services for such a great cause. It was rather nerve-wracking, I have to say—the room was full of celebrities—but it went brilliantly and we raised £750,000 that night.

I do a lot of national and local fundraising. Close to my heart are the St. John's Ambulance Brigade, the Asthma Society, Brain Damaged Adults and Children, a local hospice, and many other functions whenever I am asked. I even helped with the production of Talking Pages for the Blind.

Over the years I have appeared on radio shows helping grieving relatives, talking about my gift and giving messages from spirit to callers—a regular spot I held for two years on a voluntary basis, and also on television, helping to find missing persons.

On top of that, I still appear in many spiritualist churches across the region as guest speaker, and I have designed and produced my own birth sign and bereavement cards.

Being able to help those who are bereaved is without a doubt the most fulfilling part of my work. In October 2000, my close friend and secretary Julie came to me for a reading. I didn't know her at the time, but the events that followed were to give us a deep bond: they would also give me a new spirit guide.

Julie's sister Jackie was suffering from breast cancer. I wasn't aware of this, although I had given Jackie readings in the past. She had come to me regularly between 1991 and 1997, at which point she moved out of the area.

Jackie was a lovely woman and we had hit it off immediately, although we hadn't kept in touch in the three years that had passed. I had no idea about the bad luck she'd suffered since: it only became apparent when her sister Julie came for her reading.

Immediately, I was given the image of breast cancer. I saw Jackie's marriage breaking down, and spirit told me she had returned to Halifax just months before this reading. Then, I saw that the cancer had spread to her brain.

Unlike me, Julie was aware of her sister's illness, but had no idea of the severity of the situation. I, however, knew it would be fatal.

It's always very painful and difficult passing on these kinds of messages. Julie and Jackie, although they weren't on speaking terms at the time, were incredibly close. I was unsure how to break the news.

"I'm afraid I can see Jackie's health deteriorating," I began. "And I know you've had a fallout. But you know life's too short for these silly squabbles, and you have to see her and patch things up."

Julie looked shocked, but asked me to continue.

"The cancer has spread to her brain," I said. "And I'm afraid her time here is limited. Please put your differences behind you."

Julie took my advice, immediately picking up the phone when she returned home to make peace with her sister. But their relationship was cut tragically short when Jackie passed over in December—just two months after Julie's reading.

In the six weeks before she left this plane, Julie and her mother moved in with Jackie to nurse her through her final days. During that time the sisters talked regularly about the spirit world, and discussed how they would get a sign to each other that life really is eternal.

Julie asked Jackie to come back and reassure her that she had reached her destination and that she was okay. Unbeknownst to me, it was decided on that I would act as the medium: Julie would come to see me for a reading when she was ready to communicate.

Three months after Jackie passed, Julie decided to contact her sister. Halfway through the reading, I paused. *What a strange message!*

"This is very odd," I began. "But Jackie is holding her hands out to me. She's saying, '*Look at my nails Bridget, aren't they lovely? Tell Julie they still are, even now. She'll know what I mean.*'"

To my surprise, Julie burst into tears.

"What is it?" I asked quickly.

"I used to paint her nails for her while she was ill," Julie sobbed. "It was one of the things we decided on when we were talking about bringing messages through."

Julie told me she had already felt her sister around her, and had smelled Jackie's favourite flowers—freesias—in the air on numerous occasions.

From then on, Jackie came through to me frequently: first giving messages to pass to Julie, then helping me in other readings I was giving. She now works with me on a regular basis and never lets me down. Jackie usually steps in on the younger readings to give advice to the client and myself. She's an amazing friend; it's just a pity we only grew close once she'd passed to spirit!

CHAPTER 16

I can communicate with spirit as often as I want; they listen to me whenever I need them and it comes automatically. Even if I'm in conversation with somebody else, spirit can talk to me and I can hear them as clear as day.

If a spirit is trying to connect or I am struggling to decipher a message, one of my guides—Harry, Dad, Betty, or Jackie—will step in to help.

My day starts with me thanking God for my life, my gift, and my family and friends. I ask what this new day will bring and for help to achieve everything I need to do. I then tune into spirit to see what's going on. Usually, everything is going to plan and I know that I am fulfilling my destiny.

The year 2008, however, was my *Annus Horriblis*. Although it gave me a lot of joy at times, it was also a very painful year where I lost lots of wonderful people.

In the New Year, everything was fantastic. My brother Charlie, who had been diagnosed with skin cancer in 2005, had been told he was in remission. It was such a relief, the best Christmas present we could have had. Charlie had gone to Gran Canaria for five weeks with his wife, Anne, to celebrate the good news with their son Peter, who had settled there six years previously.

Shortly after Charlie and Anne returned on the 25th January, I was on my way home from an appointment when a message came from Harry to tell me there had been a tragedy in the family.

"*It's already happened, you'll be contacted soon.*"

Fearing the worst for Mum or Charlie, I rushed home with a pounding heart and picked up the phone to call Julie, who always knows how to calm me down in a crisis.

She wasn't in, but while speaking to her husband, Tim, our call was interrupted. I could sense a presence on the line, but I only had one telephone and knew immediately it was a sign from spirit.

"Sorry Tim, I need to get off the line," I said quickly. As soon as I replaced the handset my mobile rang. It was my brother Fergie.

"Anne's died," he informed me in a shaky voice.

At fifty-seven years old, Anne was a size eight and walked everywhere; she was very healthy. She had been with Charlie since she was seventeen, and although everyone had said it wouldn't last, they had been happy for forty years and had three children together.

Anne had gone out to work after the holiday to Gran Canaria and never came back. She'd suffered a major heart attack on her way there and passed instantly.

The whole family was devastated, none more so than Charlie, as you can imagine. He did struggle to cope, but was very brave and carried on as best he could despite his heartbreak.

Leaning over his beloved wife's coffin at the funeral, Charlie's voice cracked as he whispered something that will stay with me forever.

"I can't live without you, Anne. But don't worry, I'll be joining you within a year."

My eyes welled with tears when I heard this and I prayed his wish wouldn't come to pass: he had just been given the all clear, after all.

In the following months, spirit told me that four young people I'd had the pleasure of knowing would pass over very close together. I tried to prepare myself, but the news made me very anxious.

On the 8th July, Tom, a six-year-old boy with a very rare illness that I had fundraised for, and the father of his friend from the hospice, Michael, thirty-seven, both passed to spirit on the same day. I'd fundraised for Michael's little boy Joshua too, and I was distraught that he had lost his Daddy and Tom's family had lost a beautiful little boy.

My grief was probably compounded by the knowledge that I had two more tragic passings to come. Sure enough, in August and October of that year, two old friends of mine lost their respective son and niece—both were in their twenties, and both passed with sudden brain haemorrages.

On top of that, a close friend in Ireland developed bowel cancer, and my brothers Johnny and Billy, who still live with Mum, became depressed as the burden of looking after her became too much. I felt like the glue holding the family together, and my nerves were shattered.

More bad news followed on the 5th December, when Charlie collapsed at home and was found by his daughters Tina and Joanne. Initially, the doctors thought it was a stroke, but tests showed he had a fatal brain tumour. The whole family was overwhelmed with grief. To think Charlie had recovered from skin cancer, lost his beloved wife, and now had another terminal disease seemed so unfair. But I couldn't help thinking of the promise he had made to Anne at her funeral … *Don't worry, I'll be joining you within the year.*

Charlie went into the hospice and talked openly of how scared he was. I tried my best to comfort him but although he trusted my work, belief in the other side didn't come so naturally.

A few days later, Anne's spirit came to me.

"*I will be there for him to help him pass,*" she told me. "*Tell him not to be afraid, I'll come to him when it's time.*" I promised to pass her message on. "When Anne comes for you, you'll be ready," I assured Charlie, tears spilling down my cheeks. "She'll take you with her, and there will be nothing to fear when that time comes."

On the 2nd January, Charlie told me that Anne had come to his bedside, smiling and serene. "You were right, Bridget," he told me. "I'm not scared any more." He looked so peaceful and happy.

My brother left this world three days later, just weeks before the first anniversary of Anne's death. His promise at her graveside had come to pass.

I'm a firm believer in riding life's ups and downs, and despite the grief and hard times, 2008 also had its rewarding moments and joyful occasions.

First and foremost, my first grandchild was born on the 6th May. Elizabeth and her partner, Matt, named him Lennon Charles, and I am overjoyed that my father and brother's name lives on into the next generation—not to mention it being the name of Elizabeth's twin in spirit.

Also in 2008, I lost seven and a half stones after battling with my weight for years, and Mathew designed a new place for me to conduct readings, just over the road from my home. Everyone who walks through the door for appointments comments on its light and peaceful atmosphere. It really is tranquil and relaxing, a perfect haven for connecting with spirit.

I also took on Julie as my personal assistant, to cope with the ever-growing demand for readings. She's my best friend and an absolute star, very professional and great at her job—I've never been one for emails and all the technology related to my appointments, so it leaves me free to get on with what I do best!

And, of course, this book became a reality when I took on Sophie, my ghostwriter (no pun intended!) to write my life story. Just as she was completing the manuscript in summer 2009, a year of hard work almost over, I went to spiritualist church one evening and was overjoyed with the message I was given.

"I want to come to you," the speaker said, nodding in my direction. "Your Dad is here," she said. "He's wearing a flat cap and grinning from ear to ear—he's saying he's been reunited with his son."

I nodded. "Yes," I confirmed, smiling. "That sounds about right!"

"They share the same name and they are helping you from spirit," the speaker went on. "Your brother says to tell you it's just like you said it would be. He's with his wife, Anne, and he's at peace. He wants me to thank you for making his last few days so reassuring—there really was nothing to fear."

My eyes filled up and I struggled to contain my relief. It doesn't matter how many times I hear that—even the fact I give the same message to people every day of my life—it never fails to make me cry when it's from someone I love.

"Thank you, I feel so much better knowing that," I whispered, brushing away tears.

I was ecstatic to hear from Charlie. He has yet to come through to me; it can take some time before spirit are ready and able to communicate, but as always there are reasons for this and I'm sure the pair of them had their own for choosing to speak through the lady at church rather than come to me directly. Spirit works in mysterious ways!

I slept like a baby that night. Then another funny thing happened, that very same week.

I went to visit Mum, as I do on a regular basis. She's eighty-nine now, and suffering from the early signs of Alzheimer's.

I'd received a message from Jackie earlier in the day, telling me that Mum's medication was wrong and needed checking out.

"Hello, Mum," I said chirpily as I came into the room.

"Hello, daughter," she replied. This pleasantly surprised me; the week before she hadn't known who I was.

"Do you know who I am?"

"Of course I know who you are," she barked. "You're my daughter. You take good care of me."

I smiled. "How are you feeling?"

"I'm just fine," she told me. "Everyone thinks I'm daft, but I'm not. I know what's going on."

I was confused. "What do you mean, Mum? What's going on?"

She waved her hand dismissively.

"Oh, you might think you're the only one with the gift; the only one who gets messages," she told me coolly. "But I get messages too. I get lots of messages."

I sat up straight: this was news to me.

"Really? Who do you get messages from, Mum?"

She looked around the room for a while until her eyes fell on a picture of the Sacred Heart of Jesus.

"I get messages from the Lord God Almighty." She proclaimed.

I looked at Johnny, Billy, and Kenn, who all looked as baffled as I was.

"That's great Mum," I told her. "What do the messages say?"

She looked at me, as if wondering whether she should confide.

"I got a message saying all these pills and potions are wrong," she said eventually. "They're not doing me any good at all and you need to tell them, because I'm not taking them any more."

I sat open-mouthed. Mum and I had been given the same message as Jackie had passed to me. How could that be? All my life she had denied the existence of spirit and their messages. I'd always had my suspicions she communicated with Dad, and certainly the stigma over my work had eased slightly over the years, but Mum is a devout Catholic and has never fully accepted my gift.

So this revelation—such a long time coming—is very important to me. And while I regret it's taken fifty years for Mum to admit there is another world and that she can access it too, I feel hopeful that she might finally make peace with the path I've chosen before her time on this earth comes to an end.

Epilogue

Mum's words just go to show that we all have the sixth sense; it is something that can be developed as long as we are open to it. And whether we attribute those messages to spirits and guides, guardian angels, simple intuition, or God himself, it is doubtlessly a gift to humanity that should always be taken seriously and embraced by all of us.

I believe that every single event in my life—the good and the bad—have a reason for occurring at a particular time, and because of this faith I honestly wouldn't change a thing if I had to live my life again.

The hardest lesson of all was knowing I would lose Dad, and of course dealing with my grief when the messages finally came to pass. But although I found it incredibly difficult to accept he was taken from me, I was given confirmation throughout that painful time that life is eternal.

So when people ask me how I feel that spirit put that on my shoulders at such a young age, I always answer that I was blessed to be given messages that other family members were not able to take any comfort from. I think children are far more adaptable than adults, and my suffering was lessened to a degree by my ability to connect with the other side.

When my life on Earth is complete, I hope that I will have left a lifetime legacy and that my family will be proud of my communication with the spirit world, knowing I have fulfilled my destiny.

I know that my gift has helped thousands of people throughout my life, but it is not something I take for granted, and I can only hope that I will continue to be blessed with an ability that offers comfort to those who seek me out.

I would like to end with some questions I am often asked, in the hope that I can inspire any readers who need some reassurance about my work and the spirit world.

HOW CAN YOU REASSURE PEOPLE WHO ARE GRIEVING THAT THEIR LOVED ONES ARE SAFE AND HAPPY?

My message for anyone who is grieving for a loved one would be to say that a memory is taken from the Earth to spirit, as well as the fond memories kept here on Earth by the people who are left behind. This is the case in whatever circumstances that may be, whether the loved one be an infant or an elderly person.

Children do grow up in the spirit world, and this includes babies who are miscarried or delivered as stillborns; quite often they are given names in the afterlife.

There will always be someone waiting to assist those who are passing over, even if you can't think of any loved ones who are already on the other side. Never spend your time worrying that those you grieve for are alone in the spirit world—they are not!

Animals have souls that live on too, and many spirit people have told me that they have met up with their cat, dog, or whichever animal it may be.

As far as dealing with your pain, I remember my coping strategy when Dad passed. I used to visualize my heart with four chambers, and imagine the grief I felt flowing into one of these. Then I would picture a key being turned, locking the anxiety away. That way, he was always in my heart, but I refused to let his loss spread further than that small place deep inside of me.

I am often asked what happens when we re-marry after the loss of a spouse. Who do we spend our eternal life with once we pass over? The simple answer would be to avoid thinking in human terms.

All negative emotions we experience on this plane—anger, jealousy, bitterness—don't translate once we are out of our earthly shells. The soul carries none of this baggage, and it is entirely possible for a person who has passed over to spend their time on the other side with several partners!

I want readers to trust me when I say that no matter how bad your life is or whatever you endure, you can make it positive. But nobody is going to do it for you—you have to find the will within yourself, and banish negativity by asking for help from the other side. Above all, keep your faith, your hope, and your belief that time really does heal all.

You'll find one of my poems at the end of the book. I hope it will bring some comfort to anyone who has been bereaved.

DO WE ALL HAVE GUARDIAN ANGELS
OR SPIRIT GUIDES?

When people are in danger or having great difficulty with life in the material world, they very often say they have felt a loved one in spirit intervene to help them. I have lost count of the number of times people have said "I felt that my guardian angel was with me today."

As for the difference between angels and guides, it's a little trickier to answer. Many people feel they are being watched over by a being who isn't known to them on the Earth plane, and there are thousands of cases where a stranger—looking perfectly human—might appear in your life to help you or pass on a message (just like the lady at the garden centre!).

Was she an angel or a spirit lady? Is there a difference? It's impossible to know, but I would say that all these things will become clear when we pass, and until then we just need to know we are all protected and loved.

My guides are my Dad, Harry, Betty, and Jackie. Because my guides all lived at different periods in history, and because they all know me in a different capacity—Jackie as a confidante and friend, Betty as a mother figure and fellow spiritualist, my father as a daughter he wishes to protect—I feel I am able to turn to them individually and for different viewpoints, depending on the advice or help I need at the time.

WHAT ARE YOUR THOUGHTS ON RELIGION?

I do believe in God and I pray every day. I would say that my Catholic roots are very much a part of my life, and it would be true to say that once a Catholic, always a Catholic.

When I am in Ireland, I do go to the church every Sunday. I feel at peace there and I would imagine that when my time comes to pass over to spirit, the church at Straide would be the place where I would want to be given my last rites. Catholics believe that *out of dust was I made, and into dust shall I return*, and the idea that we will meet up with our loved ones again is deeply ingrained into my faith. For that reason I don't feel it is incompatible with my work.

However, ever since I sneaked out of church and began my path in the spiritualist movement, my eyes were opened to the fact that God is everywhere, and I began to realise that I didn't need a man in a dog collar to act as my middle man!

I'm proud of the fact my parents brought me up to believe, and I brought my children up with the same faith. But I have given them the freedom to choose their own paths. The most important thing for me is to teach them to give, to be good people, to believe in a higher power, and also to ensure they know there will always be somebody there to comfort them.

Morals can be taught without being part of a specific religious faith, and in any case, all the world's religions teach us in one way or another to love our neighbours and do unto others as we would have done to us. It's just a shame that these simple words of wisdom are so often overlooked by the supposedly faithful, and that so many wars have been fought in the name of religion. I believe we should live and let live: *As you sow, so shall you reap, As you do, so you are, As you think, so shall you become.*

DO WE ALL HAVE THE ABILITY TO COMMUNICATE WITH THE OTHER SIDE?

Although I personally believe that being a clairvoyant medium is a rare gift, I would maintain that all human beings have the capacity to communicate with their loved ones in the spirit world by sitting in silence, sending out their thoughts, and waiting for a reply.

This reply may take the form of a mental image, words in your mind that are not your own, sensing a presence, or a clear sign that you've been heard—like a flickering light, or a sudden breeze in the room.

But, as the saying goes, Rome was not built in a day— and we have to remember that our loved ones (especially those who have been taken tragically) need time to adjust in the Spirit world before they are ready and able to communicate.

Above all, you have to believe in yourself and the existence of that other world. You also have to believe that spirit can help; they don't judge or let us down. They give us openings all the time, but look out for them because they are never given to you on a plate!

We are also given many obstacles and challenges throughout our earthly lives. These are there for a reason, whether we understand them or not. We learn and grow from them, and they are crucial to our development as spiritual beings in these human forms.

I was lucky enough to be born with a highly developed sixth sense, but I believe with faith, practice, and an open mind, we can all be part of a spiritual revolution. Imagine how full of love the world would be if the skeptics and warmongers tuned into their inner voices a little more often! We really could be a global village, living in peace and harmony with our fellow man.

With love, light, and heartfelt blessings to you all,

Bridget

ACKNOWLEDGMENTS

I am grateful to all those featured in this book for their permission and cooperation, in particular my friends Julie Beaumont, Tom Howley, Breda Holloran, Marion Walsh, Rita and the rest of the Deacy family, Noreen Coleman, and the Gaughan family—especially Evelyn and Martin, who took me under their wings like another daughter, and my family, the Knights.

Thanks also to my local spiritualist church in Sowerby Bridge, and all the church officials who have kindly asked me to speak over the years. Huge gratitude must go to my spirit guides—Dad, Betty, Harry, and Jackie, without whom I couldn't do the work I do. All my love also to my wonderful family: Kenn, my husband; Mathew, Elizabeth, and Marcus, my children; and Lennon, my beautiful first grandchild, for all their support over the years, And to all of you who have come to me in the past for personal readings, audiences, and fundraisers—you are the reason I was given this gift to share.

Thank you to Tom Hennigan, for his fantastic heritage museum in Killasser, Swinford, County Mayo. Also for his enthusiasm, knowledge, and for going over and above the call of duty—he'll know what I mean! Thanks to the National Museum of Ireland Country Life, at Turlough Park, Castlebar, County Mayo, and last but certainly not least, everyone in Straide and the Copper Beech pub—especially landlord Brendan Maloney—who has shown me the true meaning of Irish hospitality!

Huge thanks also to everyone whose stories have appeared in this book, their names changed to protect their identities.

I would like to thank Connie Hill, Amy Martin, and Steven Pomije at Llewellyn Publishing for their help and encouragement, and a special thanks to Carrie Obry.

Finally, I would like to dedicate this book to my beloved father, Charles, and also my mother, Bridget, who has shown me the meaning of true strength.

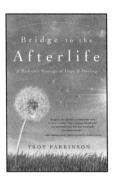

Bridge to the Afterlife
A Medium's Message of Hope & Healing
TROY PARKINSON

What if you could talk to the other side? What would you say? And what messages would the spirits have for you?

Spiritual medium Troy Parkinson, a rising star in the paranormal world, shares fascinating first-hand stories of his communications with the spirit realm.

Channeling spirits was the last thing that Troy Parkinson ever thought he'd do. A North Dakota native and self-described "ordinary guy," he first attended a spiritualist meeting when he was a college student in Boston. After receiving a message that night from his grandmother's spirit, he decided to pursue mediumship training through the world-renowned First Spiritual Temple of Boston. Parkinson now travels around the country, doing readings for large audiences and presenting workshops that teach people how to develop their own spirit-communication abilities. Troy's moving story and amazing messages from spirit will touch your heart, inspire your soul, and remind you that your loved ones are always with you.

978-0-7387-1435-6, 240 pp., 6 x 9 $15.95

Spirits Out of Time

True Family Ghost Stories and Weird Paranormal Experiences

ANNIE WILDER

Annie Wilder presents a fascinating collection of true family ghost stories and lore, brought to life with vintage family photographs. From her Irish great-grandpa outsmarting the death coach coming for his daughter Maggie, to her great-grandma seeing a falling star each time one of her children died, these personal vignettes illuminate the mysteries of the spirit world.

This collection of spirit stories includes accounts of a haunted hotel, a magical bookstore, and a faceless little ghost girl who haunted Annie's mother for decades. *Spirits Out of Time* also features protection rituals and a ceremony that readers can use to honor their family in spirit

978-0-7387-1440-0, 240 pp., 6 x 9   **$15.95**

You Are Psychic

DEBRA LYNNE KATZ

Learn to see inside yourself and others. Clairvoyance is the ability to see information—in the form of visions and images—through nonphysical means. According to Debra Lynne Katz, anyone who can visualize a simple shape, such as a circle, has clairvoyant ability.

In *You Are Psychic*, Katz shares her own experiences and methods for developing these clairvoyant skills. Her techniques and psychic tools are easy to follow and have been proven to work by long-time practitioners. Psychic readings, healing methods, vision interpretation, and spiritual counseling are all covered in this practical guide to clairvoyance.

978-0-7387-0592-7, 336 pp., 6 x 9, **$16.95**

True Hauntings

Spirits with a Purpose

Hazel M. Denning, Ph.D.

How do ghosts feel and think? Do they suffer? Does death automatically promote them to a paradise, or as some believe, a hell? In *True Hauntings*, psychic researcher Dr. Hazel M. Denning recounts the real-life case histories of the earthbound spirits—both benevolent and malevolent—she has investigated. She also explores spirit possession, psychic attack, mediumship, and spirit guides.

978-1-56718-218-7, 240 pp., 6 x 9   **$14.95**

Don't Call Them Ghosts
The Spirit Children of Fontaine Manse—A True Story

KATHLEEN MCCONNELL

A true ghost story that will give you chills and warm your heart.

In 1971, the author and her family moved into a historic home known as the Fontaine Manse. Two days after moving in, she and her husband had an extraordinary experience that left them with no doubt that unseen residents occupied the house, too.

This is the true story of how Kathleen McConnell came to know and care for the spirit children who lived in the attic of the mansion—Angel Girl, Buddy, and Baby. From playing ball with Kathleen, to saving her son Duncan from drowning, the spirit children became part of the McConnell family in ways big and small. Finally, a heart-wrenching dilemma triggered an unexpected and dramatic resolution to the spirit children's plight.

Don't Call Them Ghosts is an inspiring story of the transcendent and lasting power of a mother's love.

978-0-7387-0533-0, 264 pp., 6 x 9   **$13.95**

The Happy Medium
Awakening to Your Natural Intuition
JODI LIVON

What is it like to be a medium? Now is your chance to learn from a pro! With wit and candor, intuitive coach Jodi Livon shares the hard-won wisdom she's acquired on her fascinating journey as a psychic medium.

Over the years, Livon has helped clients, friends, family, and the dead find healing and learn life lessons. These true and incredibly touching stories not only illuminate spirit communication, but also offer guidance on tuning in to your own intuition. By relating how she receives and interprets psychic impressions, Livon shows firsthand how the psychic process works. With tips on trusting your senses, maintaining emotional balance, staying grounded, and interpreting signs from the universe, *The Happy Medium* can help you ignite your natural intuitive insights for higher awareness and guidance in life's decisions.

978-0-7387-1463-9, 312 pp., 6 x 9   **$16.95**

To order, call 1-877-NEW-WRLD
Prices subject to change without notice
Order at Llewellyn.com 24 hours a day, 7 days a week!

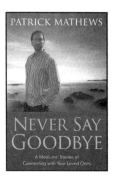

Never Say Goodbye
A Medium's Stories of Connecting with Your Loved Ones
Patrick Mathews

"I'm a normal guy . . . I just speak to dead people."

When he was six years old, Patrick Mathews came face to face with the spirit of his dead Uncle Edward. As an adult, Mathews serves as a vessel of hope for those who wish to communicate with their loved ones in spirit.

The stories Mathews tells of his life and the people he has helped are humorous, heartwarming, and compelling. Part of his gift is in showing the living that they can still recognize and continue on-going relationships with the departed.

Mathews takes the reader on a roller coaster of emotional stories, from the dead husband who stood by his wife's side during her wedding to a new man, to the brazen spirit who flashed her chest to get her point across. You will also learn step-by-step methods for recognizing your own communications from beyond.

978-0-7387-0353-4, 216 pp., 6 x 9 **$15.95**

Growing Up Psychic

From Skeptic to Believer

Michael Bodine

Foreword by Echo Bodine

What's it like to grow up psychic—in a family of psychics?

Michael Bodine was only seven when his family made a shocking discovery: he, his mother, and his siblings—including his sister, the renowned Echo Bodine—are psychic. What was it like to grow up in a house teeming with ghosts and psychic experimentation, contend with a mind-reading mother, befriend a spirit boy, and hunt ghosts with his sister Echo? And what happens when Michael's psychic talents become more of a burden than a blessing?

From adolescence to adulthood, this gripping memoir chronicles the wondrous, hair-raising, hilarious, and moving moments in Michael Bodine's life, punctuated by an ongoing struggle to come to terms with the paranormal. Discover how he rebounds from drug and alcohol dependency and learns to accept—and embrace—his unusual gifts.

978-0-7387-1961-0, 312 pp., 6 x 9   **$16.95**

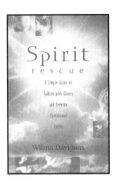

Spirit Rescue
A Simple Guide to Talking with Ghosts and Freeing Earthbound Souls
Wilma Davidson

From centuries-old battlefields to present-day disasters, Wilma Davidson has coaxed countless earthbound spirits—confused children, loyal soldiers, malevolent entities, and stubborn Titanic passengers—to "the Light." In recounting her extraordinary experiences, she brings warmth, honesty, and humor to a subject often avoided and misunderstood: death.

This revealing testimonial to the spirit world aims to create awareness, offer credibility, and bring comfort to those who fear crossing over. Davidson's poignant and insightful stories fill in little-known details about ghosts, animal spirits, non-human entities, near-death experiences, angels, and reincarnation. The author also introduces an entire cross-section of the paranormal—spiritual healing, psychic protection, dowsing, astral travel, feng shui, geopathic stress—and gives practical advice for those who wish to follow in her footsteps.

978-0-7387-0907-9, 360 pp., 6 x 9   **$12.95**